FAITH AND POWER

FAITH AND POWER

Christianity and Islam in
'Secular' Britain

Lesslie Newbigin
Lamin Sanneh
Jenny Taylor

First published in Great Britain in 1998 by
SPCK, Marylebone Road, London NW1 4DU

British Library Cataloguing-in-Publication Data

A catalogue record for this book is available from the British Library

ISBN 0-281-05153-4

Typeset by Wilmaset Ltd, Birkenhead, Wirral
Printed in Great Britain by
The Cromwell Press, Trowbridge, Wiltshire

To be an intelligent and principled participant in the dialogue of contemporary and intellectual life, the Christian must have a firm sense of the history behind present disputes and a clear idea of the relevance of Christian doctrine for the arguments of the day.

Roger Lundin, *The Culture of Interpretation*

Contents

Preface

The writing of this book is the product of a concern shared by the writers over a number of years for the articulation of a Christian vision for our society. The immediate context is the British scene, but we believe that what we have to say has wider relevance. We are particularly impressed by the issues being raised in our increasingly pagan society by our Muslim fellow citizens. In the face of the manifest signs of fragmentation and moral confusion in British society, we find ourselves bound to confess that the whole question of religious identity which Islam articulates is a question which the Church ought to have been articulating. We are convicted of having allowed the Christian witness to be so domesticated within British culture that it has ceased to be heard as the radical message that it is.

Perhaps our specific concern may be illustrated by contrasting what we have written here with the document *Changing Britain*, a report prepared ten years ago by the Board for Social Responsibility of the Church of England and accepted by its General Synod. The writers of this report were concerned that the Church should make its appeal to the widest possible consensus on moral issues which could be found among the people of many faiths and ideologies who now constitute British society. It eschewed reliance on texts (such as the Ten Commandments) and doctrines which belonged specifically to the Christian, or – more broadly – to the Judaeo-Christian tradition. The stance of this report is indicated by the following words from its preface:

> We could have contented ourselves by addressing a clear Christian message to any who might care to listen, and we do not under-estimate the value of such statements from faith to faith. Our choice of a different method reflects our concern to say things which we believe have validity for the whole of our society.

In the body of the report, therefore, the effort is made to articulate a moral vision which can be accepted by people of all religions or of none. The present work is based on quite different beliefs. We believe that the Christian gospel, with all its uniqueness and specificity, has validity for all people and that failure to recognize the crucial significance of religious beliefs is causing and will continue to cause confusion, misunderstanding and alienation at all levels of national life.

Our argument is directed, in the first instance, to Christians. We seek to show that the idea of a secular society is proving inadequate for the protection of religious freedom, and that the multiculturalism society claims to profess demands a new religious sensibility in the public space. Christians are now required to do some fresh thinking about how a society that was once shaped by Christian symbols can again be revitalized through the gospel and its bearing on contemporary political and social responsibilities.

We have been drawn together in attempting this task by various experiences during the past few years. We come from different backgrounds. One of us is a missionary, one is a scholar in the field of world religions, and one is a journalist. We are grateful for many friends who have helped us in the thinking and practice which have led to the present work. Each of us is solely responsible for the contents of our respective contributions.

LESSLIE NEWBIGIN
LAMIN SANNEH
JENNY TAYLOR

Part One

The Secular Myth

Lesslie Newbigin

I

Multiculturalism and Neutrality

To ask the question 'What kind of Britain?' is to bring into focus a cluster of concerns and anxieties which shape a great deal of contemporary discussion. Behind the questions that are constantly debated about our role in Europe, about national sovereignty, about our ethnic, cultural and religious identity and about the 'values' which should govern conduct, there lies the fundamental question what kind of a people are we, what ought we to be?

The older people among us – there are an increasing number – remember their school days when it seemed much clearer. We had a clear sense of our identity. The history we learned gave us a clear picture of who we are and of our place in the world of nations. We were (as we thought) a leading power among the nations of Europe, at the advancing edge of a world civilization which was destined to shape the future of the world. Whether our political opinions were on the right or on the left of the familiar spectrum, we had the confidence of a race accustomed to rule. We were, most people would say, part of a great Christian civilization.

There are, perhaps, pockets of rural Britain where something of this perception survives. For those living in our big cities (and they are the majority), the picture is very different. We are a multiethnic, multi-religious and multicultural society. The histories our children learn in school (and these are a much diminished part of the curriculum) are not coherent but vastly diverse. Whether at school or in mosque, temple or gurdwara, children learn many different histories and are shaped thereby into different identities. There are agonizing tensions. Is the primary self-understanding of a

Muslim child that of a member in the great worldwide house of Islam, or that of a British subject owing primary allegiance to the Crown? And is a child of British descent right to feel pride in Britain's history and achievements, or is this an offence against the world's citizenship which we must all learn to embrace if we are to survive?

The first option, pride in British achievements, is difficult to sustain in the general climate of disillusionment about the achievements of Western civilization which Britain shares with the rest of Europe. Signs of a general loss of confidence in the future are not hard to find. One recent news item may serve to make the point. The overhead sections of six motorways built less than half a century ago as part of the new network of motorways are already showing signs of collapse. By contrast, the great bridges and viaducts built in the eighteenth and nineteenth century by such great civil engineers as Telford and Brunel are still carrying heavy traffic and are objects of authentic beauty. This is sad testimony to a loss of confidence in a long-term future.

Britain has now followed the example of the United States in responding to the issues raised by ethnic mixing. Immigrants to the USA are required to go through a rite of incorporation into the society of the host country, including an oath of allegiance to the established order as defined in the constitution. They have been required to learn the language and the history of the United States, and most have been eager to do so. The aim, shared (until recently at least) by both the host country and the newcomers, has been assimilation into the dominant society, and (again until recently) this has been widely successful.

Britain has not, in general, followed this pattern. There has been debate between those who saw assimilation as the obvious path and those who, out of respect for the cultures and religious beliefs of the newcomers, desired to do everything possible to enable them to preserve their distinct identities. The ideal of pluralism,[1] of a multicultural and a multi-religious society, has been set forward as one which should command the endorsement of a nation with a strong commitment to liberty.

Indeed, there would have been difficulties in any British attempt to follow the American model. It is not very clear to a newcomer what would be involved in professing allegiance to the host country. Unlike almost all other nations, we have no national day on which all citizens are solemnly reminded of the nation's history, of the ideas which have shaped it, and of the principles for which it now stands in the world of nations. On the occasions when, as a resident in Switzerland, I have participated in the celebration of the national day, I have found it a very moving occasion. The only annual event in the British calendar which even remotely resembles a national day is when, on 5th November, we commemorate an event which did not happen and which, if it defines anything, defines us as anti-Roman Catholic.

Even the national flag, sad to say, no longer provides the needed symbol for our national identity. On the many occasions when we see a procession through city streets carrying the Union Jack, we know (and it is deeply wounding to see it) that we are witnessing a particularly vicious kind of sectarianism.

Finally, there is the person of the Sovereign as the focus of national identity. Consecrated at her coronation in a Christian liturgical action which defines her authority to rule in Christian terms, she is the most powerful symbol of national identity. But the link between the Crown and the Christian faith is widely regarded as a mere survival which has no contemporary force, and this focus of unity, once so powerful, has diminishing significance.

What exactly do we mean when we talk about a multicultural society? If the term 'culture' is used as it is widely and improperly used to include race and religion, it is questionable whether it can have any sustainable meaning. In fact, people of one race may include diverse cultures and religions, and people of one religion can embrace a vast variety of races and cultures (as does Christianity). If the word 'multicultural' is used in its loose (and improper) sense, it would seem to denote a society with now commonly acknowledged norms of belief and behaviour. (I use the word 'acknowledged' rather than 'accepted', for all societies are full of people who acknowledge norms but frequently flout them.) As Alain Finkielkraut has argued in his brilliant little book *The Undoing of Thought*,[2] the end product can only be a 'multicultural' individual who is adrift in a sea with no horizon in any direction, a landscape with no landmarks, no fixed points by which the traveller could plot his route.

There is plenty of evidence to support this prognosis. It is true, of course, that in every age people, and especially old people, have complained that society is degenerating, that 'the old days' were better, and that 'society is going to the dogs'. But, allowing for this bias, surely only a fool can deny the evidence of disintegration in contemporary British society. The inexorably rising levels of violent crime cannot be wished away. The enormous growth of the traffic in drugs primarily for the demands of the 'developed' countries, the further twist to the rising spiral of crime which this engenders, and, above all, the loss of all sense of meaning and direction, of which the demand for drugs is a symptom: all this is evidence of disintegration to which only a fool will shut his eyes.

I don't want to be blind to the elements of good in the multicultural agenda. There is much to be learned and much to be gained in the mutual interaction of cultures. If we are speaking of such matters as art, music, literature, dance, architecture, styles of food and dress, language and proverbial wisdom which are to be found in such manifold variety among human societies, there is indeed much room for mutual learning. Any society which tries to seal itself off from influence by other cultures is in danger of death. Like all living entities, human societies maintain their existence through constant interaction with their environment, including interaction with surrounding societies. In this interaction a living entity has both to receive and also to maintain its own identity. A society maintains its identity if there is within a proper balance between the conservatives who want to hold fast to old ways and the radicals who are eager to embrace the new. A society can lose its identity by too much clinging to tradition and by too readily abandoning it.

But if 'multiculturalism' is extended to the fundamental beliefs which hold a society together and provide it with the basis for the norms which control the life of its members, then it can only lead to disaster. It is here that we have to ask the difficult questions about British society.

No-one can fail to notice the frequency with which the word 'values' now appears in our public discourse. Our leaders in all walks of life speak about the importance of values, and of the need to inculcate values in the minds of the young. Parents are anxious that their children should acquire good values. Even clergymen, who ought to know better, join in the chorus. But it is hard to know what kind of reality these 'values' have. It is almost universally assumed that these values are matters of personal choice. They belong to a different order of being from the world of 'facts', which are not matters of personal choice but which are those things which we have to accept whether we like them or not.

I remarked earlier that all living entities survive by a constant interaction with their environment. This requires learning about what that environment in fact is. Living creatures survive and flourish only if they are able to find out what in their environment is dangerous and what is sustaining. It has been shown that even such a lowly creature as an earthworm can learn to avoid danger and seek safety. The same applies to human societies. They cannot survive and flourish by the aid of self-chosen values. It is necessary that they learn the facts about their environment, facts about which it is possible to be right or wrong. The language about 'values' obscures the fact that, in general and in the long run, the way people behave depends on what they believe about the real world. There is, thank God, a vast range of matters in respect of which we can exercise freedom of choice without danger of self-destruction, and this freedom makes possible the rich tapestry of varied cultures, which in our newly discovered global city we are free to explore to our great delight. But there are also matters in respect of which we do not have freedom to choose with impunity. The Ten Commandments are, from one point of view, the product of a particular culture at a particular time in history. They speak, nevertheless, of matters on which one cannot exercise free choice without the risk of disaster. In these matters it is not appropriate to talk about 'values'. There are matters in respect of which a society cannot remain neutral, merely holding the ring for the free exercise of personally chosen 'values'.

Can a society or a state be neutral? In an early work entitled *The State in its Relation with the Church*, W. E. Gladstone argued that the state is a moral entity capable of doing right or wrong and responsible for doing right.[3] Since these moral judgements cannot be divorced permanently from belief about what is the case, Gladstone argued that the state has an obligation to acknowledge the truth –

the truth of the Christian religion. This, for Gladstone, included the obligation to tolerate dissenting opinion. In later years, as is well known, Gladstone moved to join the advancing tide of liberalism, but the argument of his earlier work is still, it seems to me, hard to refute. Britain is still, nominally, a Christian state. The Sovereign is consecrated to her office in a Christian act of worship. She is pledged to uphold the establishment of the national churches of England and Scotland. The proceedings of Parliament are opened with Christian prayer. Christian language, symbols and traditions are intertwined with our public life at every level. But many, probably a majority, regard these as anachronisms, touched perhaps with a pleasant nostalgia, but essentially irrelevant to the present life of the nation. Are we committed to the idea of a neutral society?

2

The Undoing of Secular Society

In May 1939, T. S. Eliot delivered three lectures in Cambridge under the title *The Idea of a Christian Society*, published later that year with the same title.[1] By the time the lectures were published, Britain was at war. What were we at war for? Technically, to prevent Germany from invading Poland, an obvious impossibility; actually, as a result of the slowly awakened realization that the whole future of European society was at stake. During the preceding decade, sunk in deep economic recession, British people had been very slow to realize that the rising movements of Fascism and National Socialism were much more than a passing phase in democratic politics. Only very slowly (and almost at the last minute) both those in power and ordinary people began to grasp the fact that an earthquake was happening which could bring the whole of Western civilization as we had known it to ruin. It was a fight about two different visions of human society. It was not a war for territory, or for markets, or for raw materials: it was a war between two fundamentally opposed beliefs about human nature and destiny. It was a war for the soul of Europe. Neutrality was impossible.

In such a conflict it is necessary not only to know what we are fighting against, but also to have some vision of what we are fighting for. I do not think that Eliot's book had any wide influence in shaping the public mind, but there was much seeking after some vision of society in which the Christian faith would have a shaping influence. Under the leadership of William Temple, J. H. Oldham, William Paton and many others, and through the creation of the British Council of Churches and the publication of the *Christian*

Newsletter, there was an effort to shape a vision of the future of the nation illuminated by the Christian faith. On a larger scale, the popular 'Religion and Life' weeks drew large numbers of people together in all parts of the country. After the close of the war and through the hard deprivations of the immediate post-war years, there was a strong conviction that a different kind of Britain was possible, a Britain freed from the poverty, hunger and disease of the past. The immense achievement of the creation of the welfare state at that point is proof of the power of this vision. In the minds of many of its architects it was their way of putting into effect the idea of a Christian society.

But the vision faded and the effort flagged. With rising prosperity came the first symptoms of what we now call 'consumerism'. The general election advertisement which told the voters 'you have never had it so good' and illustrated this with a picture of a table laden with rich food and wine, was perhaps the most notable summons to a different lifestyle. The message spread quickly. Consumerism soon carried all before it, and the welfare state had not been designed with defences against this tidal wave. It had been conceived in a time when good citizenship was understood to mean, or at least to include, such ideas as self-restraint and self-sacrifice for the common good. It began to look as if there was no limit to the possibilities of affluence. New technologies and new global economic arrangements enabled the developed world to increase its wealth at a speed previously undreamed-of. It would not be until this bonanza had run its course for a couple of decades that the twin threats of ecological disaster and human polarization dawned on the consciousness of the affluent society.

The tentative explorations of the idea of a Christian society could not continue in the new circumstances. Indeed there was deliberate and even violent reaction against such ideas. The staggering achievements of human technology which had made possible the reconstruction of the ruined cities of Europe and the vast increase in the wealth of the 'developed' world prompted a burst of confidence in the power of human technology. The decade of the 1960s was a period when, as at the time of the Renaissance, there was a surge of pride in the power of human beings to control their environment and to solve their problems. The decade opened with the promise of President Kennedy to put a man on the moon within ten years, and this bold assertion of human power was to be the distinguishing mark of the whole decade. Its most prominent legacy has been the tower blocks in our cities, built, as the architects of the time explained, not for pragmatic but for ideological reasons as symbols of the fact that we are no longer mere creatures crawling around on the ground like other animals. It was the decade in which a much misunderstood Dietrich Bonhoeffer was endlessly quoted to the effect that man has now come of age and can live 'as if God did not exist'. It was the decade of *The Secular City* (Harvey Cox), of *The Secular Meaning of the Gospel* (P. M. Van Buren) and, above all, of J. A. T. Robinson's *Honest to God*, with its assertion that the idea of God in any traditional sense is no longer acceptable to 'man come of age'. Man, apparently, was to be celebrated as secular man with no need for religion.

Characteristic of the decade, therefore, was the publication of *The Idea of a Secular Society* by the Christian economist D. L. Munby. His thesis, which had a prevailing influence in ecumenical thinking about social issues at the time, was a direct rebuttal of the thesis of T. S. Eliot. So far as I know, it still represents the views of most Christian people in this country. British society is generally understood to be a secular, multicultural and multi-ethnic society, in which many religions coexist, and should coexist on equal terms. We are, it is generally understood, a secular society.

But we are not comfortable with this creed. Does a secular society have no norms, no accepted beliefs about what is right and what is wrong? The word 'norm' originally referred to something given as a standard by which things are measured. We have two adjectives derived from it: 'normative' and 'normal'. The first suggests an objective criterion by which behaviour could be judged; the latter suggests the average in a range of possibilities. 'Normal behaviour' thus means 'what most people do'. In a society shaped by the Bible and the Judaeo-Christian tradition, the 'norm' is to be found by attending to this tradition, and the 'normal' behaviour of a society is to be judged by this standard. It does not itself furnish the 'norm'.

But a secular society, by definition, eschews any such appeal to divine revelation. Does that mean, then, that the state is, in direct denial of Gladstone's view, neutral on moral issues? The state, every state, punishes crime, but has it total discretion to decide what shall and what shall not be regarded as crime? The dilemma of the secular society was well illustrated when in response to a strong current of feeling in the nation about the need for 'values' in national life, the prime minister announced the slogan 'Back to basics'. This was immediately seized upon by opponents as a suggestion that the government was concerned about moral standards and there was a hasty retreat. But does a government not have a duty to represent, uphold and advocate high moral standards? Or do the principles of democracy require that governments simply reflect whatever is 'normal' in society? The ambiguity of the present situation is highlighted by the avidity with which the press (financed by the tastes of its readers) celebrates the discovery of moral lapses among those in public office. If one understands the moral law as expressing the personal will of a good and wise and merciful God, one can recognize that a person may sincerely seek to do God's will and yet fail, thus needing discipline, forgiveness and restoration.

But if one has come to believe (as we have largely come to believe since the eighteenth century) that the only realities with which we actually have to deal are those 'objective facts' which science investigates, then our profession of moral conviction will be understood as a cloak for our real interests. 'This alone I know with certainty' wrote Freud, 'namely that man's value judgements are guided absolutely by the desire for happiness, and are therefore merely an attempt to bolster up their illusions by argument.'[2] Thus, when those who have made profession of high moral ideals are found to have acted in contradiction to them, public opinion seizes upon such happenings with a joy and enthusiasm which shows that they do not really believe what they have professed. For if moral claims are merely a cloak for self-interest, moral lapses would be a matter of course which should evoke no surprise – certainly not the shouts of moral indignation which follow 'revelations' in the gutter press. The public appetite for sordid 'revelations' demonstrates the power of moral passion which is denied its proper context in a holistic understanding of the world and of the human situation within it. If, as the ideal of a secular society requires, all claims about divine revelation are excluded from the domain of public political discourse, there is no secure basis for moral judgement. There is only the 'normal', understood as average behaviour within a given society at a given time. There is no benchmark against which that 'normal' could be assessed. There are plenty of examples, some of the most terrible belonging to this century, of whole societies sinking into a situation where the 'norm' is, by biblical standards, the criminal.

There is much pessimism in British society today. The confidence which so impresses us in the Britain of the nineteenth century has ebbed. We no longer believe that continuous progress towards a better life for all is to be expected. And there are solid grounds for this pessimism. It is true, of course, that there is and has always been among older people a nostalgia for a supposedly happier past, and this is a fact which must be reckoned with. But three things cannot, I think, be denied. The first is the growth in violent crime. The second is the huge expansion in the sale and use of drugs. The third is the development here and in other 'developed' countries of an 'underclass' – something totally different from the 'proletariat' of Marxist doctrine. These latter were a powerful force upon which capitalist society depended for its survival. The new reality is the growth of a class of people effectively outside the economic system. As in other European countries, there is a hard core of people who have been unemployed for a long time, and of young people who have never had paid work and have no expectation of having paid work during the rest of their lives. These include, of course, many from the ethnic minorities. It is obvious that this must generate a sense of alienation from society and must undermine any sense of responsibility for the welfare of society as a whole. The long-term effect is compounded by the fact that fewer young people are now nurtured in stable families in which two parents, father and mother, can both fulfil their essential roles in shaping the character of the child. All serious thinkers on the matter agree that it is in the family that a child learns (or fails to learn) interdependence of rights and obligations, the very stuff out of which stable moral commitments are developed. As fewer and fewer children have this foundation experience, there are fewer parents able to pass it on in their turn to their children.

These intertwined and mutually reinforcing factors in society – family disintegration, alienation, drugs and crime – add up to a situation which the secular society seems unable to tackle. It is true that we still inherit (with the top of our minds) the basic conviction of the Enlightenment, that every problem has a solution, that humanity is capable of solving its problems without divine aid, that advancing technology will 'crack' the problems that still baffle us. But there is less and less to sustain this belief. No economic programme is yet on offer which could solve the problem of long-term unemployment within the parameters of the present global economic and financial structures. The attempt to curb the rise in violent crime by tougher policing and more prison sentences seems to be counterproductive. The USA, with a prison population of around 1 million, has more violent crime than any other developed country. The international traffic in drugs, fuelled by the ever-increasing demand of the 'developed' world, continues to grow in spite of international attempts to stop it. And fewer and fewer children are born into stable two-parent households.

It does not seem that the secular society is capable of creating the 'values' for which it seeks. Attempts to develop a convincing morality on purely secular assumptions have not succeeded. In the end, people's behaviour will be governed by what they believe about the real world. If human behaviour is only a matter of self-chosen 'values', there are no grounds requiring me to accept obligations other than those which are in my interest. In our contemporary secular society almost all moral conflicts are fought in terms of 'rights'. But 'rights', like 'values', have no existence outside a wider understanding of what is the case, of what is the reality with which we have to deal. 'Rights' exist only within a juridical framework in which there is an agency which acknowledges an obligation to meet the demand for a right. Otherwise 'rights' have no real existence. As long as 'rights' dominate public rhetoric to the exclusion of 'obligations' society can only disintegrate.

To raise the question of obligations is immediately to be confronted with the central figure of the European Enlightenment of which we are the heirs: namely the figure of autonomous rational man. The dynamism of that movement which launched Europe on a career of world domination arose in large part from the liberation of the human mind from tradition, especially religious tradition, in order to exercise freedom of choice untrammelled by any obligation to a more than human reality. Characteristic of all religion is the imperative to worship, to bow down in humility and adoration before something greater than the self. In most parts of the world, human communities, cities and villages, have – often as their centre – a place, temple, mosque, church, set apart for this purpose. In the secular society those are perceived as anachronisms. They belong, it would seem, to the kind of society we thankfully left behind a long time ago: the deferential society, the 'upstairs downstairs' society where everyone knew his (and especially her) place and we 'looked up' to our betters. To express reverence, or even respect, for one's 'superiors' is seen as an offence against the basic truth that we are all created equal, with equal rights to whatever is going.

And disillusionment with our 'superiors' is deepened by the manifest failure of the institutions of the secular society to solve the problems which I have referred to above. It seems to be a necessity of the democratic process that those seeking the votes of the electorate have to promise solutions to these problems. But it becomes increasingly clear that the remedies do not work. The resulting scepticism and cynicism about our political institutions reinforces the conviction that our 'betters' are no better than ourselves. This is, of course, simply one element in the general disillusionment which has followed from the inability of human society to fulfil the utopian promises of the Age of Reason.

It was in such an atmosphere of cynicism and disillusionment that, in the period following the First World War, Fascism and National Socialism were born and became, with incredible rapidity, the monsters that almost destroyed European civilization. At the present time something even more unexpected is happening. Religion, which the Enlightenment had confidently assigned to the margins of society where it could no longer control public policy, has re-entered the political arena in force. Religious fundamentalism, especially what is commonly termed 'Muslim fundamentalism', is now one of the major issues in international politics. The idea of the secular society is, in a way unimaginable even a few years ago, facing an all-embracing challenge to its legitimacy.

3

The Rise of Religion

It is common to hear the names of Darwin, Marx and Freud listed as those who have done most to shape the thought of the 'modern world' though it may be doubted whether, in the long run, they will be seen to have effected the sort of irreversible change in human thinking which is commonly attributed to them. But it is arguable that the name of Max Weber, the German sociologist, should be included in any such list. His theory of the inevitable and irreversible secularization of society has, arguably, done as much as the work of the other three to shape our assumptions about the society we share.

Weber argued that the continuing and increasing application of rational calculation to all aspects of human life would have the necessary effect of marginalizing religion. This would be seen in the worlds of industry and of management in all its aspects. The application of science-based technology to industry would have the effect of making the individual worker simply a replaceable unit in a machine-like operation. Analogous processes would operate in the development of bureaucracy, whether in the business of government, or in industry, or in voluntary societies. The factors which shape the face-to-face relationships of human beings to each other (and this is the area where religion has its home) would be more and more replaced by impersonal relationships in which each human unit has to perform the functions which the rational organization of the whole requires. As more and more people are caught up in the workings of these machine-like organizations, in which everything is planned to operate with the necessity of a well-constructed machine, there would be less and less room for such ideas as providence, miracle, the supra-natural. There would be a 'disenchantment' (*Entzauberung*) of the world. Religion might still operate in the world of the home or the small voluntary community, areas in which these principles of mathematically calculated rationality do not apply. These could only be at the margins. They would have a diminishing place in the drive towards ever new achievements of rationality. The area in which religious ideas are still credible must shrink. Secularization is an inevitable and irreversible process.

Because something like this has been the accepted wisdom of the Western democratic societies for most of this century, it has been difficult for its peoples to grasp the significance of the contemporary rise of religious fundamentalism. The most dramatic example of what we have now to consider was the revolution which toppled the government of the Shah of Iran and replaced it with that of the Ayatollah Khomeini in 1979. The British Ambassador in Tehran at the time is reputed to have expressed the opinion that this event would, in the perspective of later historians, rank in importance with the French Revolution of two centuries earlier. Yet the event went practically unreported in the Soviet press at the time. When churchmen from England questioned Soviet officials for the explanation of this strange silence, the reply was to the effect that the event could not be reported because it was impossible to explain it.

A similar incomprehension was apparent in Britain when the storm broke over the publication of *The Satanic Verses*. In the Muslim community there was burning anger against what was perceived to be blasphemy, whereas in the most liberal opinion in this country blasphemy had ceased to be a word with any real meaning. It was said to be something concerned with protecting 'the Christian religion'. Since, for the purposes of public discussion, God does not exist, the idea that to blaspheme his name is a terrible offence does not occur to the mind.

For many in the liberal tradition, the rise of religious fundamentalism has to be explained on psychological grounds. It is a reaction of fear. It is the retreat of frightened and bewildered people into the safety of a fortress of unchallengeable dogma. It is the attempt to escape from difficult questions. There is no need to deny that there may be some truth in these explanations in some cases. But one does not dispose of truth claims by psychoanalysis, except in the society which has ceased to believe in the possibility of knowing the truth. If we are not all to retreat into the 'non-realist' bunker where disagreement is impossible because there are no facts about which we could disagree, then one must listen to the truth claims made by religious fundamentalists and formulate our response. We have to take note of the fact that it is precisely in those societies in which the programme of secularization has been most vigorously pursued that the fundamentalism has developed. And we must be open to the possibility that the programme of secularization, for all its visible successes, fails to take account of realities in the long run.

The term 'fundamentalism' is more often used as a term of abuse than as a self-description. From the point of view of the 'enlightened' liberal, a fundamentalist is a person whose mind is closed to anything which does not accord with perceived religious dogma. It is, for the purposes of ordinary conversation, a synonym for 'bigot'. When originally coined by Christians in the United States it conveyed the conviction of Christians that the rationalism of the Enlightenment had led Christians to surrender fundamental matters of belief in order to accommodate the supposed requirements of 'modern' thought. It has been particularly concerned to affirm the authority of Scripture. Oddly (but perhaps understandably), it is deeply committed to two typical products of the Enlightenment, namely a fervent nationalism and equally fervent commitment to the system of *laissez-faire* capitalism. Hindu fundamentalism is also passionately nationalist and (unlike Christian and Muslim fundamentalism) has no worldwide ambition. Japan, the most spectacular example of ultra-rapid modernization, has in Shinto a religion which is at the same time essentially nationalist. But it is significant that, following the rapid modernization of Japanese society, there has been an explosive growth of new religious movements, broadly in the Buddhist tradition, which now claim the allegiance of one-fifth of the population.

From a global perspective, however, by far the most significant manifestation of religious fundamentalism is in the Islamic world. Muslim fundamentalism is now a major factor in world politics, and may perhaps be the dominant force in the coming century. Islam does not, and cannot, accept the role of a 'religion' in the sense which that word has in contemporary English usage. It cannot accept relegation to a margin of life as one element among many. Islam stands for the global submission of all human life everywhere and in all its aspects to the revealed will of Allah. It therefore embraces all the spheres which 'modern' Christians identify as juridical, political, cultural, economic. It is transnational in its vision of human society. Through the Organisation of Islamic Conference it forms a very important unit of international political power. Its representatives vote as a bloc at the meetings of the United Nations. In so far as Islam is able to realize its aim of universal solidarity, it represents the most extensive political unit in the modern world, stretching from the Atlantic to the Pacific. It has behind it the history of a brilliant civilization which for many centuries far surpassed that of Christendom. And, as it emerges from the centuries during which it has been humiliated by the colonial expansion of Western Christendom, it offers to the secular societies of the West a vision of an order established by the revealed will of Allah. Muslims in Britain are well able to see the vacuity of the secular society, the absence of any firm basis for the much desired 'values', the drift towards meaninglessness and hopelessness manifest in the explosion of the drug market, and the inability of existing political parties to address these root causes of our malaise. To the question 'What kind of society?' our Muslim fellow citizens have their answer. Through the network of mosques (now more than 2,000 in the UK) and through the teaching which is there provided for their young people, Muslims seek to maintain the integrity of their society in a world which they (with much justice) perceive as pagan. The firmness of their stance contrasts with the relative timidity with which Christian leaders occasionally challenge the norms of British society. It is indeed of much ironic significance that commentators have noted that the proposal to portray Jesus as one of the characters in the TV show *Spitting Image* had to be vetoed because of the indignant protests not of the Christians but of the Muslims. Christians' protests can be ignored, not those of Islam.

4
Conclusion: Coercion and the Cross

The vigour of the Muslim challenge to the contemporary secular society is surely something which ought to awaken the conscience of Christians. There is a great body of Christian opinion in Britain, probably representing the majority of professing Christians, which cherishes the idea of a secular society, fearing that any alternative would eventually lead us back to the horrors of the religious wars. This is a very understandable fear, especially in the light of a growing public recognition of the plight of Christian minorities in Islamic countries.

At this point it is important to draw a distinction between two senses in which the word 'secular' is used in these discussions. Those of us who were part of the Christian community in India during the early years of independence were wholly committed to the concept of a secular state in the sense of a state which would provide full freedom for all the different religious beliefs. This is the concept which is now challenged by Hindu fundamentalism. But the adjective 'secular' can also be used to denote a set of beliefs which claim that the whole cosmos is intelligible without any reference to supra-natural realities. There can be a secular state in a profoundly religious society such as India is, but the secular society is frequently, and perhaps generally, conceived in terms of the second meaning of the word 'secular'; that is to say it would denote a society in which belief in God could play no part in public debate. It is, I think, arguable that the secular societies which have developed in western Europe since the Enlightenment have been able to survive because of the very strong residual

Christian element in the European tradition. Whatever may be the language of the public forum, the sense of the reality of God and of his commandments, and of Jesus and his saving work, is still so widely diffused in the European mind that it has protected us from drawing the full logical conclusion to the secular thesis. It was, as so often, the philosopher Nietzsche who drew attention to this obvious conclusion: if there is no God, everything goes. The issue has been raised in India by one writer known to me, Mr Chaturvedi Badrinath, who has pointed out the calamitous consequences of the translation of the English word 'secular' into Hindi by putting the negative in front of the word *dharma*. *Dharma*, as he argues, is the constitutive element of the ordering of the universe and has to be the constitutive element for the ordering of human life. To translate it as religion is very misleading. To use its negative as the translation of 'secular' is to affirm that the secular society is set loose from any all-embracing governing order, something which, as he rightly points out, can only lead to total disaster.

A similar confusion is involved when the concept of a secular society is understood to mean a society ruled by the ideology of secularism, or, to use what is perhaps a better term, of naturalism. That is to say the belief that nothing exists except what is measurable, quantifiable, perceptible by the senses. It is this naturalist philosophy which tends more and more to take control of the public square in the Western secular democracies.

This is greatly reinforced by the development of the mentality of consumerism. It is more and more accepted as axiomatic that every person has the right to make his or her own choices, even in the most fundamental matters, and that any interference with this freedom is an offence against human dignity and autonomy. In contemporary Western society the main foundation for this assertion of freedom is the belief that ultimate truth is unknowable and therefore all opinions are equally worthy of respect since in the last analysis all of them are matters of personal choice. This means that public issues are finally settled by numbers and power. The majority rules, and the way is open for totalitarian claims, whether political, cultural or religious. The liberal society, with its absolutization of freedom, has no defence against those who use its freedom to destroy it. Eventually the question of truth is unavoidable. In the foundation documents of the American Republic the liberty of the individual is described as an endowment given by the Creator. This appeal to a supra-natural source gives it a place to stand in the flux of uninhibited liberty, but if that source is disallowed there is simply no logical reason why the opinion of a minority, or even of an individual, should be accepted as truth against the claims of the majority.

In our present situation in Britain where Christians and Muslims share a common position as minority faiths in a society dominated by the naturalistic ideology, we share a common duty to challenge this ideology, to affirm that it can only lead our society into disintegration and disaster, and to bear witness to the reality of God from whom alone come those 'norms' that can govern human life, that *dharma* which can give order to the chaos of human passions. Here, as I have suggested, Christians should be both encouraged and challenged by the much more vigorous testimony of Islam.

During their long histories, both Christendom and Islam have sought to establish the absolute hegemony of their faiths over whole societies. Christians have, for the most part, been so chastened and humiliated that they have learned the bitter lesson and should never again be tempted to go down this road. It is not clear that Islam has been through the same experience. What is becoming clear, as I shall argue later, is that in the last analysis it is only the gospel that can provide the basis for a society which is free, but in which freedom does not lead into disintegration and destruction. The reason for this lies in the unique character of the gospel itself. It is in the fact that God's decisive revelation of his wisdom and power was made in the crucifixion of the beloved Son, that in his resurrection from the dead we have the assurance that, in spite of all appearances, God does reign, that in the commission to the Church we have responsibility to bear witness throughout history to its end that God does reign, and that until the end God has provided a space and a time in which the reconciliation of our sinful race is possible, not by coercion but by freely given faith, love and obedience.

At this moment in the discussion, however, the point to be emphasized is that which is shared between Christians and Muslims. In contrast to the prevailing ideology of naturalism, both Christians and Muslims affirm that the great reality is God and that God has made known his will for the human race, and that that will must be decisive for all human living, public and private. This is a direct contradiction of the ideology of naturalism. The triumphs of this ideology have been founded upon the undoubted success of the methods of science in achieving an astounding expansion of human knowledge of the natural world and of human power to interfere with its operations for our benefit. That particular kind of human knowledge, which we have come to designate by the word 'science', is that kind of knowledge which is obtainable by the use of empirical observation and reasoning. We have learned what a vast amount can be discovered by these methods as they have been more and more refined in the recent history of science.

But there is one question which these methods cannot answer because they do not ask. It is the question about purpose, about intention, and the reason for this is simple. By the methods of empirical observation and reasoning it is possible, within limits, to discover the causes which operate in the natural world, and therefore in some measure to control them. What cannot be discovered by these methods is the purpose, if any, for which all these things exist. And the reason is that purpose, intention, are personal categories. It is only living persons who have purposes, intentions. Until these intentions are fully realized they lie hidden within the minds of those whose purposes they are. Only at the end, when the final result has been achieved, can we discover by observation and reasoning what that was. Until then we must remain ignorant, or else we must ask the one whose purpose it is, to tell us. And if we are given this information we shall have to accept it in faith, which will depend upon the trust which has been evoked in us by the one who tells us. Short of the end, there will be no final, demonstrable, proof.

It is, of course, possible that this cosmos has no purpose and that it is simply a neutral entity upon which we are free to impose our own conflicting purposes. That is, for practical purposes, the belief of most of our Western secular societies. Most people will simply have to accept the world as an enigma, and human history as a meaningless farce. Occasionally there may arise a Napoleon, a Lenin, a Hitler, inebriated by power and confident of ability to shape the whole of history to their purposes. But the end is always the same.

In so far as the naturalist ideology excludes from the public square any appeal to divine revelation, it renders impossible any publicly accepted doctrine of the purpose for human life. And by the same stroke it eliminates any possible ontological, factual, basis for moral judgements. If the purpose for which a thing exists is unknown, the adjectives 'good' and 'bad' cannot be applied to it. It may be good for one purpose but bad for another. These adjectives must drop out of public use. They are only expressions of personal preference. They refer to no objective reality, but only to what are called 'values'. When rejecting these assumptions Muslims and Christians are at one. One could wish that Christians had been as confident and clear in their unmasking of this folly as Muslims have been. Christians have reason to be grateful to their Muslim fellow citizens for this service, but they are also under obligation to re-examine their own recent record, to repudiate their too easy accommodation to the assumptions of a secular society, and to seek afresh a vision for the future of a society shaped by the Christian gospel.

Part Two

Islam, Christianity and Public Policy

Lamin Sanneh

5

The West's Reluctant Re-education

The recent irruption of fundamentalist Islam into public consciousness in the West has all but upset the long-established understanding of the harmonious relationship among church, state and society. Muslim political activity has disrupted the old arrangement in which the Church left to the political sphere issues of the public realm on the basis that a socially responsible public realm is the fruit of Christian teaching. The churches lost their clout when centuries ago they relinquished to the national state the instruments of power, though the habit survives of viewing the churches still as repositories of power. It does not take Muslims long, though, to find out that the churches no longer count politically. Many people in the West are still slow to recognize the challenge in the Muslim view of religion as power, for as recently as the 1960s the Muslim presence in most parts of the West occasioned little interest among public officials.

As new immigrants in search of economic opportunities, it was widely believed that such Muslims and their children would be absorbed into the Western global economic mainstream and assimilated into society. In so far as Muslim religious life is concerned, that could safely be relegated to the domain of private piety and as a matter for the parish. Although there were indications even then that Muslims wished to have an active say in wider public issues such as education and in the design of the school curriculum, no more attention was paid to them than was compatible with the secular status quo.

Muslim educational needs, Western leaders felt, could be met within the existing provision for religious instruction in schools, and since comparatively few public-sector schools observed any religious rite to speak of, Muslim participation would thus result in secularizing their religious habits, too, so that their assimilation into society would progressively weaken their clamour for religious recognition and thus remove any need to deal with it. Thus what was left of the reduced flow of Muslim immigration into the West after immigration controls had been applied could easily be neutralized by secular domestic forces on the principle that one more Westernized Muslim would make one less religious person. Muslims would reinforce Western secular norms. They should accordingly be welcomed as secular allies.

That has not happened, or has not happened in the way envisaged. Consequently, we are faced instead with a Muslim resolve to make Islam count in the public realm: in schools and universities, in the upbringing of children, in marriage, divorce, property, inheritance, taxation, banking and trade. Central to Muslim demands is the desire to give the state a role in enforcing religious rules, including blasphemy laws. If a Western secular state is thus agreeable to protecting Muslim religious interests, then to all intents and purposes the secular state qualifies as a surrogate Sharī'ah institution and may as such be deemed *halāl*. In these respects, Muslims will have succeeded in turning the state into convertible religious currency, charging it with responsibility for Islam and judging it by that supreme criterion. It will have mattered little that Christians have long repudiated the state as a religious organ, for Muslims would fill the space thus abandoned.

Apart from Western misunderstanding of Islam as a politically friendly religion, we have the additional problem of misunderstanding the Muslim transformation of the secular state, a transformation in which the state acquires moral infallibility by becoming a funnel for the norms of Sharī'ah. The state thus ceases to be religiously indifferent. In fact the state ceases to be a limited political liability. By the same token, a state-sponsored religion ceases to be transcendent truth or moral absolute, for political force will have replaced freedom of conscience.

These and other consequences follow from Christians having abandoned or lost the habit of believing in a Christian society, and as such being unable to respond to the Muslim religious challenge in any publicly meaningful way. We do not mean by this a lack of knowledge among Christians of the Muslim religious and historical tradition, for such knowledge abounds in our colleges and universities, but that Christians find it easier and less embarrassing to conceive of Muslims in non-religious categories such as race, minority groups, economic underclass, gender and immigration. These categories qualify for public entitlement, whereas religion does not. However, since 'Muslim' is a religious designation before it is anything else, that is missed by a head-in-the-sands secular attitude. Eventually, however, Muslims make their presence felt with demands for public attention and state endorsement, and for a share of public resources. By that time they have, regretfully, learnt to leave Christians where they find them, namely, in religion as a week-end private diversion. Christians offer little encouraging example to active Muslims, so that if such Muslims wish to lay claim to the public agenda then they must often do so without the company of Christians. They must press on regardless of that fact, for that is the vocation revealed truth sets out for believers. It makes little difference that Muslims are a minority, except where being a minority secures for them the lucrative fruits of political correctness.

The West and a Multifaith Society

In his very fair and honest treatment of Muslims in Britain, for example, Eric Butterworth, writing in 1967, nevertheless speaks of British Muslims in terms of immigration and race, and of social relationships defined by ethnic origin and economic background.[1] Butterworth was rightly concerned with issues of employment, education, housing, social integration and racial tolerance, and nothing that has happened since he wrote has diminished the importance of these issues. Yet what is interesting in so much of the discussion about Muslims in the West, Britain included, is how little religion figures in it. The racial or ethnic classification that seems easy to adopt for Muslims is actually without merit in Islam. One is or becomes a Muslim by virtue of submission to God and to the authority of the Prophet, not by virtue of ethnic or racial identity.

In fact, the Qur'ān expresses it well, saying blood kinship will not avail in the final reckoning, which will be a moral one. 'Neither your blood-kindred nor your children/shall profit you upon the Day of Resurrection' (60:3), or, elsewhere: 'And no burdened soul can bear another's burden, and if one heavy laden cried for (help with) his load, naught of it will be lifted even though he (unto whom he crieth) be of kin . . . He who groweth (in goodness), groweth only for himself, (he cannot by his merit redeem others)' (35:18, Pickthall's translation). Not even family bond or the *volkgeist*, the Qur'ān insists, can replace personal responsibility or avail in the life hereafter (84:13–15). It is that urgent moral note that has animated Muslim mission in the world, securing the adherence of people on the grounds that their natural social traits are worthless and must be superseded by revealed truth lest these become falsely absolutized. One does not undertake mission in the name of kin or ethnic transcendence, for transcendence in the Muslim view is God's exclusive attribute.

How can we expect a secularized West to understand this when it regards religion as a function of material interests? Yet how can the West fulfil the expectations of its Muslim communities as Muslims without appreciating how religion is for many the source of fundamental moral identity? The secular liberal view is that it is not important what you believe so long as you are free to believe it, and that since there are so many religions, no one religion matters. But is that adequate to the Muslim claims for fundamental religious truth and the obligation to witness? Is a neutral liberalism capable of promoting genuine pluralism, when it lacks divine truth and vision at its centre? Will neutral liberalism, alas! bring us just as quickly to indifference as to tolerance? As it is, neutralism is not really viable, for it is clear you are not neutral towards the truth claims of religion if you start out with the position that those claims are less true than your individual freedom to be free of them. That merely lays a stake to freedom as self-evident. When, for example, Carlos Fuentes declared that he would stake his life to defend the right of the quest for truth but would kill anyone who claims to have found the truth, saying this in defence of Salman Rushdie and against his religious foes, he was laying neutrality on the altar of commitment. The honest course for him, and his best protection, lies in abandoning a misguided neutral and relativist position and embracing the truth that is the fount of freedom (John 8.32).

It is this contradiction that the Muslim religious challenge is exposing in the establishment status quo of secular liberalism, and the churches need to respond before it is too late. Thus the Western preference for taking cognizance of Muslims by using ethnic classification implies that religion is a function of ethnic and cultural identity, like language, racial type, tribal custom and communal tradition. Yet because the West fails to appreciate the vitality of ethnic life in world Christianity, it misappropriates it for Islam. The West is led to this by an erroneous notion that Christianity has destroyed ethnic cultures, and is everywhere incompatible with their promotion. By contrast, the West feels that Islam has protected ethnic cultures and is eminently suited everywhere to their flourishing. Yet the fact of the matter is that one can be a Chinese, a Burmese, an Ethiopian, an Egyptian, a Yoruba, a Zulu, an Ashanti, an Afik, an Idoma, a Vai and countless other variations, and still be a Christian, so that ethnic identity or territorial location ceases to define one's religious faith. Modern Christianity is thus a religion of the peoples and tribes of the world, marked by unprecedented pluralism of vernacular Scripture and liturgy and without territoriality as a unified or unifying rule. However weak our Western sense of a Christian *esprit de corps*, we should nevertheless acknowledge that the gospel has been as much an enterprise of the West as it has been of non-Western societies where it is expressed in diverse ethnic and linguistic modes. The situation in Islam is just as complex, though Muslim loyalty is based on claims of transcendence, a religious way of life supported by non-vernacular norms of Scripture and Sunnah, Qur'ān and Hadīth, of faith and practice, *'aqā'id* and *'ibādāt*.

Notwithstanding that fact, people have continued to interpret along secular lines British Muslim religious attitudes in one of two ways, either as (1) a mere reflection of the rural–urban configuration, with those from rural backgrounds exhibiting more conservative attitudes and those from towns and cities tending to be more liberal and progressive, or as (2) attitudes that will evolve in time to parallel Christian secularization, though many such Christians, finding the promises of secular emancipation largely illusory, may still be groping for religion as an emergency exit. The first way of viewing the matter places the responsibility on the process of urbanization to bring about the withering of religion, with the corollary of secular displacement, while the second way puts all the religious eggs in the basket of personal piety, investing religious capital in the desires, needs and wants of the individual person, a market-oriented way of looking at religion.

Both approaches break little new ground. The first approach echoes the primacy of the secular over religion, reflected in the claim that religious observance among Muslims tends to drop off with literacy in English and assimilation into the West. That suggests that the children of Muslim immigrants, raised in British society and educated in British schools, will eventualy shed their protective religious shield as they gain confidence in their new adopted home. In that view religion is a residual phenomenon fated to dissolve once Muslims attain social fulfilment.

In the second approach religious doctrine is sized up for its relevance and user-friendly value in filling gaps of human loneliness, personal insecurity, individual despair and moral disenchantment, but in any case religion is banished into the citadel of personal piety, where it functions as a factor of the lonely, agonized human spirit. The sentiment of religion as secular disillusionment is well expressed by Marat de Sade as follows: 'these cells of the inner self are worse than the deepest stone dungeon, and as long as they are locked, all your revolution remains only a prison mutiny to be put down by corrupted fellow prisoners'. Religion, thus, has no objective validity, only a form of subjective self-exile, and that is true of Islam. In the secular view, so long as there exists in society a religious hangover, it matters not a whit if it happens to carry a Christian or a Muslim name, for in the final analysis religious experience only expresses human need rather than being based on reliable knowledge or demonstrable truth, and will as subjective value remain outside the public discourse. It can be tolerated without public risk or cost, or suppressed as such.

Thus what is clear in this secular analysis is how little prepared the churches are in dealing with Muslims, whether with those on their doorsteps or with those with roots in traditional mission fields. The parish structure, which worked relatively well in a more or less stable society, especially for the conditions of nineteenth-century urban growth, was in the twentieth century ill-adapted to respond even to co-religionists from abroad let alone to Muslim strangers and immigrants who were now compatriots and neighbours. Second, seminary and theological recruitment and training offered very little by way of preparing men and women for working among Muslims, so that among the front ranks of those charged with guiding the churches in their engagement in a multi-faith society there was much incomprehension, confusion, hesitation, defensiveness and retreat. In the meantime, the erstwhile secure cultural base of Christian national identity was being eroded by secular forces as people sought alternatives to religion for a fulfilled life. It was not uncommon, for example, to find returning missionaries from parts of the Muslim world slipping unnoticed into remote parish appointments, or else into civic or humanitarian projects, their talent, knowledge and motivation channelled into plant maintenance or humanitarian causes. The claim often made for this kind of transfer of Christian priorities is that this world, too, is part of the kingdom of God, which justifies Christians appropriating it into the divine scheme. However true that may be, it nevertheless amounts to nothing less than special pleading in the light of the churches' own announced position of surrendering to secular realism and its scientifically orderly universe. Those who are convinced by the modernist project are likely to have made a questionable exchange of the claims of the gospel for the secular promise of universal human fulfilment. In the light of that kind of Christian compromise, Muslim religious claims have raised the stakes for Christians, challenging Christians about having paid too high a price in yielding the religious ground to a secular takeover.

Many thoughtful Muslims are concerned with what they see as the West's reckless act of allowing the religious centrepiece to be torn out of the heart of society and culture. Specifically, they react with disbelief to the dishonour that Christians have allowed to fall on the name of Jesus, who happens to be accorded an honoured place in Muslim religious life. Muslims are similarly astonished at the way Christians have 'modernized' their Scriptures as human construction, yielding completely the grounds of an operative transcendence, and in the process making Muslims unsure about whether a common cause with Christians might not be a pact with a false or subversive partner. Yet an alliance with Christians in the West ought in theory to be appealing to Muslims, for a Christian religious frame of reference has no better and more obvious affinity in an otherwise God-deficient society. However, the Christian demotion of religion as mere pious intention dismays and disappoints Muslims. While it would be naive to pretend that any hastily arranged interfaith alliances could take on the secular West in its present uncompromising mood, it is also symptomatic of the extent to which Christians have been marginalized in their own society that they have seemed incapable of seizing any religious initiative, on their own or in association with Muslims. The churches seem content in dealing with needs, desires and feelings as values worth defending, while Muslims wish to stress the importance of revelation and transcendent truth. Consequently, Muslims are justified to charge Christians with compromise, if not surrender.

Thus the irony of Christians relinquishing the uniqueness of religious claims in the interests of interfaith understanding and harmony has thus kept them out of step with the demands of religion as public truth. The argument has often been made that the claim of Jesus as the way, the truth and the life without whom there is no salvation available to human beings is in conflict with the tolerance, pluralism, inclusiveness and racial equality by which a liberal democratic enterprise is advanced, an argument that has affected the churches profoundly. As one writer asserted with uncommon confidence, the claim that Jesus is the only way to God is advanced by people who have grown up and lived in a solely Christian environment, where one never meets people from other faith communities, because if one did, it is assumed, one would recognize how absurd and ignorant such a claim is. However, as the encounter with Muslims has demonstrated, this argument is an inadequate one, perhaps even misleading. The values of tolerance, pluralism, inclusiveness and democratic liberalism are themselves derived truth-claims from Christian teaching, and commending them places us in the position of a fundamental personal commitment that is of a piece with their religious source. In any case, religion is not an environmental or a cultural trick, for were that to be the case, then Muslims, Hindus, Buddhists and others would not be spared, either, which creates the awkward situation that in one move of renouncing the claims of Christianity as backward we have declared tacit war on the unique claims of all other religions. Thus, as a matter of procedure, not to say of the West's own historical experience, we must abandon that approach to interfaith relations and start publicly with where the gospel has placed us.

One indication that a secularized society is already too religiously handicapped to respond meaningfully to the Muslim challenge is that the Muslim appeal to the political instrument is viewed by the secular West as an unwarranted breach by religious fundamentalism. In response, secular people argue that religious fundamentalism must be checked and neutralized by engaging moderate, modernist Muslims who are willing to settle with the West on terms set by the West. In other words, a secularized society knows only how to deal with religion when it has been thoroughly emasculated in the fashion of the gelding of Christianity. Yet the view that politicized religion is tantamount to religious fundamentalism does not fit with the other view that religion is merely a function of social background and economic status, destined to be made extinct with the pace of material progress. Put another way, the evidence of religion becoming durable in the secular process conflicts with the secular view of religion as an evolutionary stage. Thus the durability of religion unmasks the secular distrust of it, warning us that it is by no means safer and more enlightened to entrust a secularized society with tolerance than to return to religion as source of truth.

This is also where a strictly sociological view of Muslims is inadequate, because the Muslim insistence on religion as public truth is not simply the *métier* of a minority immigrant enclave but a demonstration of the obligation imposed by God in the service of transcendent truth. Muslims believe that the divine injunction topples all penultimate and relative loyalties, whether they be loyalties of nation, race, gender, economic class or political party. Even human agency is itself indeterminate, however necessary in the proximate scheme of things. That is why it is asymmetric to use national or geographical designations such as Britain or the West as analogues to Islam or Muslims, for that makes a national or a geographical designation equivalent to a religious or normative designation. On the contrary, the normative import of the term 'Islam' and 'Muslim' must be grasped as first order of business, and brought alongside their natural equivalents of 'Christianity' and 'Christian', which then requires us to try to determine what the normative Christian basis of cultural designations might be. To fail to do that is to set back the task of the theological transformation necessary for a multifaith society.

It may be that in the West we have long forgotten that religion and politics were once closely intertwined, since we have passed through the controversial and costly form of religious territoriality in Christendom, yet in the vital overlap of the democratic heritage with the sanctity of human life and the God-given value of personal freedom, we have a continuation of the interconnection of religion and politics. The Muslim challenge, thus, should have the salutary benefit of returning us, not to an untenable and discredited Christendom, it goes without saying, but to the truth basis of a liberal democratic society and how precisely the gospel speaks to that.

It would be an exaggeration to claim that the Western Christian response to Islam has evaded or obscured the central demand of Muslims for religion as an active player in the public arena. Nevertheless, the relative silence of the churches on his question has allowed such an impression to be formed. Furthermore, what is so striking in Christian discussions of Islam and Muslims is the preponderant view of religion as personal consolation, as a comfort blanket in a stressed, uncertain world. With that attitude, we feel it would be unfair to deny Muslims the modicum of a religious refuge. If Muslims want to resort to religion as an emergency exit in a troubled, stressful secular world, then that is their prerogative. There is no gainsaying the fact of human security and consolation finding their true answer in God's tender mercies and promises; and in that sense viewing Christianity as a look-alike Islam based on a common faith in God's sovereignty and grace, in witness and discipleship, in devotion and sincerity, and in a common mind of ethical accountability to God and to our fellow men and women, has much to commend it. It is often fired by admirable motives of goodwill and friendship, and much of it, besides, is true enough to be the abiding insights of the two great religious traditions. Yet to press that as a strategy to rescind Christian uniqueness and the public validity of religious truth-claims is to reject what is at the heart of Jesus' life and ministry, and what is also of crucial importance for interfaith integrity.

To return to Muslim political activism, it is not in the first place a repudiation of democratic liberalism, but rather of the wilful ideology that freedom, progress and equality are self-generated values, that religion is irrelevant and truth a decoy for self-interest. From the religious point of view, this reductionist attitude to religion is totally inhospitable to the comprehensive vision of truth. Muslims, therefore, see it as moral and ethical abdication, and are baffled as to why Christians do not see it that way, too. Thus what aids and abets Muslim radicalism is the irony that Western secular ascendancy, with its Christian props knocked from under it, proves at first approach remarkably soft to the Islamic counter-thrust, so that when confronted with the religious basis of Muslims' political demands, its apparently unassailable axioms of human autonomy and material determinism crumble with little resistance. There are too many cases where with little trouble Muslims have been able to circumvent the secular criticism of religion with a simple strategy, a strategy that is symmetrical in its evasiveness. Accuse Islam of not being modern and liberal enough, and Muslims would answer that it is the cultural practices of Muslims that are to blame rather than the true teachings of the Qur'ān and the Prophet. True Islam does not err. Similarly, challenge Muslim practices, say, of restrictions on gender-mixing in school, at sport and at worship, and the response is that these are cultural values which need to be respected in the interests of greater cultural tolerance and diversity. For those who reject an 'essentialist' view of religion and yet who wish to pass muster in the theatre of political correctness, this cultural argument is decisive, and offers a concession and a reprieve to Muslims, while for those Muslims who are protective of the claims of Islam as revealed truth, their 'essentialist' position is preserved by tilting at the cultural windmill. What this amounts to is exposing secularism as being susceptible to the same reductionist procedures it pioneered; and aware of that weakness, Muslims find little incentive to assimilate and succumb. In the midst of such unassimilated Muslims, the

West is left with little choice but to return to the Christian foundations of its own rich heritage, Catholic, Protestant and Noncomformist.

6

Tolerance, Pluralism and Christian Uniqueness

Lesslie Newbigin has helpfully explored the important theological dimension of the challenge of religious pluralism, and we should turn to him now. On the matter of other religions, Newbigin is sensitive to the calls for racial tolerance and cultural acceptance. In the presence of Hindus, Buddhists, Muslims and Sikhs, he says, we are reminded that our societies have become more diverse and different, and in these circumstances many people in the churches are calling for an abandonment of the policy of converting people of other faiths. The Christian faith may be true for us who are Christians already, but it is not necessarily true for others. Our confession of Jesus as Lord and Saviour and our worship of him in the language of the Church is right and proper. But we have no right in a pluralist, diverse society, critics urge, to say that there is no other name given under heaven by which we are saved. The empirical situation flatly contradicts such a claim. Modern historical consciousness, these critics say, must disallow Christian claims to uniqueness.[1] Many theologians have claimed that for Christians to offer their religion as the only answer to the global security and environmental challenge is preposterous. These theologians maintain that to affirm the validity of the other great religions of the world has become a necessary part of the struggle of their people to emerge from the spiritual and cultural humiliation of European colonialism. Furthermore, some of these critics speak of the astonishment of a Hindu at the idea that God has had only one incarnation. These critics say the Christian attempt to place the event of the incarnation in only a first-century historical record is nothing short of folly. The radical new fact of the acute sense that we are all part of one global society more and more dependent on each other is incontestable.[2]

Yet, this fact, Newbigin responds, does not mean that we are not all of us in search of truth and salvation, or that in that search we should not possess a reliable clue into universal meaning and history. It is not true that all roads lead to the peak of the same mountain. Some roads lead over the precipice. For the Christian, the ultimate clue is Jesus, the one God chose to honour and glorify the divine name, and who met that choice at Bethlehem and Calvary.

Newbigin makes the point with some force that religious pluralism, in the sense both of competing truth-claims and of simple numerical multiplicity, does not and cannot exclude claims of absolute uniqueness lest we become totally imprisoned in subjective relativism. Such relativism would destroy the validity of religion, including the religion of those we would defend. Such awareness led Langdon Gilkey of Chicago, for example, to admit with some frustration that pluralism, including the type of religiously neutral criterion some writers advocate, cannot exclude absolute claims for truth.[3] Gilkey turns to John Dewey and William James, not Paul and John, for a pragmatic solution to this problem. However, even in such pragmatic company, Gilkey still feels frustrated. Truth-claims by their nature are not some sort of convertible currency to enable us to purchase things we desire or value on other grounds, as pragmatism would have it. Truth-claims are not a question of will-power, *à la* Nietzsche: you want a collectivist society, so you produce the sacrosanct truth of the infallibility of the revolutionary vanguard and smash your way to Judgement Day. The objection of people like Gilkey that absolute truth is oppressive is not remedied by anything less than absolute truth, certainly not by an ideological pragmatism.

The oft-repeated assertion by modern critics that Christians do not possess the whole truth, that God is impartially and equally accessible through religions and cultural streams other than our own falls flat on its own face, because the claim of impartial and equal access itself behaves like a truth-claim. So it begs the question, what is the authority for our contention that we can see through a millstone as well as most, that no-one's grasp of the truth is adequate? If we make that claim on the pretext of human finitude, then we base that claim on naturalism, not on higher authority. If we box ourselves in like that, then we would have trouble defending truth-claims, including those of other religions. We would have to disallow their truth-claims, too. If, on the other hand, we made them exceptions, then, to be consistent, we must allow them to press their truth-claims and receive our submission. Thus the question persists of how we honour other religions unless such honour rests on truth-claims which for Christians flow out of Scripture and tradition.

In this regard, Newbigin speaks forcefully of what he considers a troubling reversal and denial among modern critics of the claims the Bible makes about God. When disaffected theologians speak of the Copernican revolution, of a move that amounts to the crossing of the Rubicon of religious pluralism where it is no longer feasible or convincing to assert Christian uniqueness, they do so on the basis that humanity is moving towards a common ideal and a shared historical consciousness, which is the transformation of human life from self-centredness to God or Reality-centredness. Newbigin says this is an illusion, because to claim all human beings as united in their desire and search for salvation is to leave human beings holding centre-stage, shifting the focus from God, or Reality so-called, to human needs and desires. It is, according to Newbigin, a reversal of biblical teaching. It is a shift that is the reverse also of the Copernican one. 'It is a move away from a center outside the self, to the self as the only center',[4] diverting Christian theology from a concern with the saving acts of God to religious experience as a feature of the general human condition. A new religious anthropology thus displaces the canon of revelation and salvation. Here the anthropological mouse tries to shift the mountain of faith.

By contrast Newbigin believes that Christian mission must proceed from the tension between the amazing grace of God and the appalling sin of the world, with confidence only 'in the infinite abundance of [God's] grace.'[5] It is better, Newbigin contends, to see and judge cultures by the criterion of the gospel than to allow each culture to be itself the criterion by which it judges others. Ethnocentric hubris behaves differently by pretending that modern historical consciousness has abolished the need to judge others and has left us only with the frontier of self-contained critical consciousness. We can only make value-judgements grounded in our relative, limited, isolated spheres of life. That way we reject the arrogance that we have the right to impose our views on others, but that, says Newbigin, is an illusion. 'To affirm the unique decisiveness of God's action in Jesus Christ is not arrogance; it is the enduring bulwark against the arrogance of every culture to be itself the criterion by which others are judged.'[6]

Newbigin is careful to separate this judgement from the one often posed about whether the non-Christian can be saved, whether, that is, the non-Christian will go to heaven after death. That question is God's alone to answer. Furthermore, the question is a mere abstraction, abstracting the soul from the full reality of the human person as an actor and sufferer in the ongoing history of the world. The question is not, 'What will happen to this person's soul after death?' but 'What is the end which gives meaning to this person's story as part of God's whole story?'[7] A third difficulty with that question is its focusing on the individual need to be assured of ultimate happiness, not on God and his glory. 'The gospel, the story of the astonishing act of God himself in coming down to be part of our alienated world, to endure the full horror of our rebellion against love, to take the whole burden of our guilt and shame, and to lift us up into communion and fellowship with himself, breaks into this self-centered search for our own happiness, shifts the center from the self and its desires to God and his glory.'[8]

Thus, Newbigin rejects the exclusivist position that all who do not accept Jesus as Lord and Saviour are eternally lost. In witnessing to the non-Christian, the Christian witness takes as his or her starting-point the non-Christian experience of the hearer without which there can be no way of communicating. This fact makes it impossible to affirm a total discontinuity between the Christian faith and other religions.[9]

Newbigin is, therefore, adamant that it is not our business to say who can or cannot be saved. 'I confess that I am astounded at the arrogance of theologians who seem to think that we are authorized, in our capacity as Christians, to inform the rest of the world about who is vindicated and who is to be condemned at the last judgement . . . We have to begin with the mighty work of grace in Jesus Christ and ask, How is he to be honoured and glorified? The goal of missions is the glory of God.'[10]

This leaves Newbigin free to explore human religiosity in both its historical and intellectual expression. He is critical of Christians setting themselves up as inquisitors. 'There is something deeply repulsive in the attitude, sometimes found among Christians, which makes only grudging acknowledgement of the faith, the godliness, and the nobility to be found in the lives of non-Christians. Even more repulsive is the idea that in order to communicate the gospel to them one must, as it were, ferret out their hidden sins, show that their goodness is not so good after all, as a precondition for presenting the offer of grace in Christ.'[11] On this matter, Newbigin says that Christians share the human story equally with non-Christians. We take decisions about the part we will play in that story, decisions we cannot take without regard to others who share that story. That shared commitment is the context for true dialogue, which is not about sharing religious experience, not about who is or is not going to be saved, though it may include that, but about the meaning and goal of the human story. In dialogue Christians must tell the story of Jesus, the story of the Bible, as the power of God for salvation.[12]

Newbigin's theological critique draws its power from his global sensitiveness, from his deep and long acquaintance with cultures and languages other than those of the West, but its vital core is the West and its spiritual crisis. His own personal experience of having lived for a long time in another culture, learned its language, expressed his faith in that new medium, and subsequently reflected on its implications for him and for other cradle Christians in the West, represents a crucial advantage for the multifaith needs of contemporary Western society. Thus, whether or not you agree with him, Newbigin offers encouragement to those who wish to seize the theological initiative to promote multifaith tolerance and understanding, and in that respect his challenge to the modern West is no different in kind from that of Muslims. *Les extrêmes se touchent*. (The two extremes meet.)

7
Secular Liberalism and the Muslim Challenge

As that of a Christian Englishman, Newbigin's ecumenical and global sensitiveness also shows the way religious commitment and national identity can be discerningly put to what the Quakers call 'the Christian query'. In that sense he is representative of the modern West as a legacy of Christianity, however contested that legacy may be. It is as such that the gospel has played a formative role in shaping modern political and social institutions and structures. One example of that is the pioneering role Christian thinkers played in establishing the principle of politics and religion, church and state, as valid and distinct domains in their own sphere. This separation, without precedent, was natural to Christianity because its founder, considered a public nuisance, was executed at the political altar, and because for three centuries that fate menaced Christianity as a persecuted religion. Its formative image, deeply etched in the catacombs of the empire, set it apart from the phantom of political triumphalism. The founder of the religion held no earthly political office, and in fact rejected the earthly throne and sword as unworthy of his life and example. Though Christians later came to enjoy political recognition and even power, and to believe that this was an acceptable status quo, their chequered history reminded them it was not always so. If need be, they could break with the tradition of territorial 'Christendom' and deem that their emancipation. That is how they once came to look upon secularism, and how today they may again look upon the claims of Muslim 'territoriality'.

The Church was never more involved in politics than during the era of the Holy Roman Empire, when faith and territory were joined as a principle of membership in church and state. Constantine secured the freedom of Christianity, not its establishment as an exclusive state religion. He saw himself as Pontifex Maximus, the visible earthly vessel of an all-too-misty divinity whose intuitive, malleable purpose he could attach to the robust will of the state. He claimed to be the colleague of the bishops of Nicaea, but only as a 'bishop of external affairs' and of those things in Christianity deemed useful and convenient. The real shift came only with Charlemagne, who took Christianity out of the sacristy and established it as 'Christendom', weaving it into the fabric of the state. In that scheme the political ruler was seen as God's appointed agent, the herald and instrument of God's mission. Thus political affairs and religious matters were two strands of a single fabric. It followed from this that church and state were united in purpose even though as institutions they represented different functions. While the Church had custody of the moral law, the state was concerned with enforcing the rules of allegiance and conformity that gave practical expression to the higher spiritual law. Conformity rather than personal persuasion was the chief end of religious activity under this corporate arrangement.

Christendom identified itself with territoriality in the sense of making religion a matter of territorial allegiance. Church membership was coterminous and interchangeable with territorial location, and territorial rule was established on, and made legitimate by, the ruler's professed religion.[1] In this scheme, Christianity was inevitable.

We must again stress that the tradition of separation as it developed in Christianity is unique to the religion, as is evident from the earliest records available to us where the supreme sovereign is always conceived as divine, with politics as a religious idea and religion as a political idea. This was the case in imperial Rome where Caesar was God, and in the case of the Jews, as Josephus points out, where God is supreme ruler. In Islam, similarly, God is supreme ruler, and the caliph His mere deputy. In remote antiquity the same practice obtained with the god–king identification which persisted into latter-day ideologies of divine anointing of worldly leaders. Invariably, the search for a political ideal has led to the divinization of political authority. Speaking of the ancient Chinese case, for example, Arthur Waley described how the craving for political unity produced the psychological need for an orthodoxy that combined sacred territoriality with divine authority. He wrote:

> To the Chinese of this period the word One (unity, singleness, etc.) had an intensely emotional connotation, reflected equally in political theory and Taoist metaphysics. And, indeed, the longing – or more accurately, the psychological need – for a fixed standard of belief was profounder, more urgent and more insistent than the longing for governmental unity. In the long run man cannot exist without an orthodoxy, without a fixed pattern of fundamental belief. It is hard for us to-day who live in societies, like those of France or England, which despite a surface moral anarchy, are in fact rooted upon Christian ethics, to imagine such a state of chaos as existed in China in the fourth and third centuries.[2]

The fundamental pattern of the political development of human society is the unique place accorded to a supreme personal monarch, usually exercising power in terms of a divine impersonal law. The supreme personal ruler will thus attract the worship of his or her subjects as a god incarnate, the terrestrial likeness of a heavenly potentate whose will is then translated into action in the manner of an irresistible impersonal law of nature. Dissent or resistance in that scheme becomes unthinkable, the ultimate rebellion. The subjects of such a ruler will ascribe to their sovereign credit not only for their material well-being but for personal qualities like joy and sorrow, good and evil, blessing and curse, success and failure. Conversely, the supreme personal ruler receives religious anointing as moral sanction of the political idea, as is illustrated in the famous remark of Henry IV that 'Paris is worth a Mass'. In either case, whether in the instance of a supreme personal ruler or in that of a supreme impersonal law of nature, at the level of society the outcome is the same, namely, the unity of the Universe is deemed synonymous with the unity of rulership, and vice versa. This is the seed from which religious territoriality emerged, with religious faith being a matter primarily of membership in a society where rulership is fused with territorial identity and given transcendent value. The traits of birth, soil and authority culminate eventually in religion as a national and racial rite.

It is only with Christianity, though not necessarily with all forms of it, that this iron chain of identity was broken, and broken with fateful consequences for Western history. When the time was ripe, Christianity broke decisively with what had until then been a universal norm by abandoning the view of religion as a construct of earthly power, and its converse of the state as a religious construct. Christianity took the idea of Divine Personality and fixed it in the Man of Sorrows who was bruised for our iniquity, a radical departure from Divine Personality as fixed in political fiat and force and in a holy territorial space, the divine agent, that is, as world conqueror. The divine quality thus became the transforming power of the divine solicitude instead of a human attribute hardening into a universal territorial principle. By setting itself apart from this enslaving ideology of religion as a territorial construct and the territorial construct as revealed law, Christianity shattered the chain that fettered humanity from time immemorial. With that truth secured, the way was open for undreamt-of possibilities for history and human community. That is why the irony today – of taking the fruits of that intellectual revolution and cutting Christianity out of the picture because it is deemed antithetical to political liberalism as a pragmatic enterprise – contains the trap of a tragic failure. Christian uniqueness has become an easy practice target for secular liberal shots at intolerance and bigotry, but it is that uniqueness that opened the path for progress in all domains of life, including the necessary, though regretfully not always the timely, critique of injustice and oppression in the West or anywhere else. It would, however, be consistent if from the same source of uniqueness we could prescribe for our present condition.

Although it is normal today to speak of 'the mosque' and 'the synagogue', these terms do not carry the sense of a separate domain as 'church' does in Christianity. For the Muslim or Jew the mosque or synagogue is a building, a place of prayer and worship, and of community events, perhaps, but no more. In Britain, for example, the vast majority of mosques existed in people's homes, perhaps as halls adjoining the back or side of a house. The mosque did not have the sense of an institutional structure as the church did, though in Britain pressure was brought to bear on Muslims to construct all-purpose structures as mosques. The closest Muslims have come to the church–state distinction is in *halāl–harām*, 'approved–forbidden', but even here the notion is controlled by the idea of clean–unclean, holy–profane, rather than by coeval domains of authority. Sometimes *dīn–dawlah* polarity is used to represent the church–state distinction, although here again it does not fit. *Dīn* means religion and *dawlah* means alternation, rotation, turning. In any case, in Muslim religious thought the 'secular' is an unfamiliar idea and is in fact of recent vintage, thanks to Western influence. *Halāl* and *harām* are not complementary terms: they are opposites. *Halāl* is meritorious while *harām* is taboo, implying horror and scandal. The *harām*, in fact, might be a sacred enclosure from which unauthorized persons are forbidden to enter, hence the *harīm*, the exclusive women's quarters of the house. In none of these examples, however, do we have a duplication of the Christian idea of church and state as separate but coequal domains, which then raises the question about how secular society, as a tradition derived from Christian teaching, can deal with the Muslim challenge based in religion but repudiating the rightness of separating the things of Caesar from the things of God. The short answer is that it cannot. And that, then, leaves us with a return to the teaching of Jesus and the Christian tradition, and especially to the peculiar historical adaptation of Christianity that has shaped and informed the make-up of the modern West, including Britain.

The Muslim challenge has called anew for a reappraisal of the Christian leaven in the modern enterprise by which the West finally emerged from a wretched fatalism into the glorious liberty of the children of God. That religious inspiration is the source of Christian Europe's spiritual and material achievement, and from it stemmed the consensus of church–state relations whereby the state was removed from having any responsibility for the salvation of souls and the Church from legislating for the economic and political life of society. This church–state consensus has promoted national life by recognizing that church and state are linked in the lives of people whose faith and allegiance have a grounding in moral truth as well as in pragmatic use. The community of Christians, gathered for worship and the ministry of the sacraments, and held together by ties of mutual obligation and responsibility, constitutes the prototype of the political community. The religious rule of free association carrying unavoidable obligation and responsibility anticipates its repetition in the political sphere. Thus formal separation of church and state conceals a very real reciprocity in the sphere of social and personal life, and the fact that the state may not enjoin or prescribe faith, or the Church compel conformity, does not mean that at the level of public responsibility there is not a vital connection between them, as the Muslim challenge is increasingly making clear.

However, much else came to be built on this religious foundation that resulted in weakening confidence in the God who ordained it for us. In the first place, the religious freedom inspired by the theological insight concerning the divine purpose for human life was diverted into an aggressive individualism that was exploited by the free-enterprise culture, with freedom of conscience transposed into consumer choices of the free-market system. In the second place, the consensus was converted into faith in human beings; faith in the human capacity to subdue nature, and faith that the subjection of nature will achieve human well-being. However, human dexterity with the tools of control and prediction made it easy to propagate an all-too-illusory faith in the essential goodness of human nature which will be achieved when human beings abandon superstition and embrace rational, objective truth. There thus developed the secular liberal doctrine that human history is moving inexorably towards progress and the fulfilment of human desires, a liberal credo that could not easily be shaken from its firm moorings in Darwin and Hegel, from its anchorage in the benevolent efficiency of nature or in the uplifting design of unity wrought by the universal spirit.

The upshot of this liberal faith is a secular culture in which religion is banished into the citadel of private piety, as we have remarked. Liberalism staked its reputation on faith in human progress, with the secular state as necessary machinery. Human well-being in this liberal scheme requires the state instrument and, to a degree, that we be shackled to the state. Right-wing conservatism for its part sought capture of the state to mobilize market-driven individualism and the sanctity of personal property. Thus liberals and conservatives together reinforced state power from ostensibly opposite standpoints.

This double reinforcing secular ideology has provoked Muslim fundamentalism into attacking head-on modern confidence in political ultimacy, in the state as our finality. The overriding argument being made here is to respond to the Muslim presence in our midst by reappraising democratic liberalism not just in terms of its friendliness to a multifaith society but in terms also of its roots in the Christian religious heritage. We are especially interested in assessing Islamic objections to the notion of religion only as personal faith based on private persuasion and choice, even though such a notion has in the West been fruitful of tolerance, pluralism and the birth of the secular state. Yet if religion is right in what it claims about the meaning and purpose of human life, then it cannot be banished from the public sphere entirely or reduced to the level of pious intentions, which is the Muslim contention and should be the Christian position, too, nor can it, at the same time, be co-opted as a social commodity, which is the liberal democratic tendency.

The late Ayatollah Khomeini of Iran once complained that Muslims have been robbed of their heritage through the connivance of the West. Western agents, he charged, 'have completely separated [Islam] from politics. They have cut off its head and [given] the rest to us.'[3] The reference is to the creation in Muslim countries of the secular national state as the successor to the trans-national Islamic caliphate. As we saw in the previous chapter, a similar complaint was made by Sādiq al-Mahdī, the Sudanese political leader who pilloried the secular national state for being the means by which anti-religious forces have entered non-Western societies and been fomented. He assured his bewildered co-religionists that Islam was the God-ordained answer for their undeserved ills.[4] Such sentiments have resonated with rank-and-file Muslims, in part because they invoke powerful religious symbols to compensate for insecurity among the mobile classes, and in part because they exploit widespread rank-and-file disenchantment with Western-led economic programmes. Since the modern secular state as a creation of the West stakes its credibility on the ability to deliver economic fulfilment, the failure to bring material security to the majority of its citizens has exposed it to the damaging effects of religious criticism, thereby seriously undercutting its authority. Thus the appeal of religion reflects this rising disaffection with the West almost as much as it draws upon Islam's canonical tradition, or what is claimed for it.[5]

In terms of that tradition, modern Muslim views on political legitimacy have their roots in the Prophet's own personal legacy in Medina and Mecca, where he established territoriality, *dār al-Islām*, as the handmaid of religious faith.[6] It was not long before the early Muslims were rallying round the political standard, *lā hukm illā bi-illāhi* ['no government except under God'].[7] The words have echoed down to our day, refined and mediated by the mediaeval theologian, Ibn Taymiyya (d. 1328), as a stringent theocratic credo. A contemporary Muslim writer cites an identical opinion from the second of the Four Righteous Caliphs, 'Umar ibn Khattāb (d. AD 644), to the effect that 'There is not Islam without a group, no group without power (authority), no authority without obedience. If someone is made master on the basis of jurisprudence, this will be for their and his good, and if he is made master otherwise [say, by a secular constitution], this will be destruction for all of them.'[8] However, it is from Ibn Taymiyya, among others, that modernist Muslim reformers in the last two hundred years have received their marching orders, from Jalāl al-Dīn Afghānī to Sayyid Qutb and Ayatollah Khomeini.

In view of Ibn Taymiyya's influence on modern critical Muslim assessments of the West, a few words are in order on his ideas. He spoke about the indispensability of God and the Prophet in political affairs, what he calls *siyāsah ilāhīya wa ināba nubūwīya* ('divine government and prophetic vicegerency'). He contended:

> To govern the affairs of men is one of the most important requirements of religion, nay, without it religion cannot endure . . . The duty of commanding the good and forbidding the evil cannot be completely discharged without power and authority. The same applies to all religious duties (holy war,

> pilgrimage, prayer, fast, almsgiving), to helping those who are wronged, and to meting out punishment in accordance with the legal penalties . . . The purpose of public office is to further the religion and the worldly affairs of men (*islāh . . . dīnahu wa-dunyahu*) . . . when the pastor exerts himself in proportion to his ability to further both, he is one of the most excellent fighters on the path of God.

'The exercise of authority', he concluded, 'is a religious function and a good work which brings near to God, and drawing near to God means obeying God and his Prophet.'[9] Thus authority is the possession of moral truth.

These are uncompromising words that impute territoriality to religious orthodoxy, words that would make Muslims discontented with a merely secular pragmatic political ethic. Yet they are words that also make it difficult to coexist in a pluralist society. One way out of Ibn Taymiyya's rigid scheme is to make 'the duty of commanding the good and forbidding the evil' (*amal bi-ma'rūf wa nahy 'an al-munkar*)[10] the basis for a theocentric view of the world rather than the justification for a theocracy. A theocracy would ironically still be the rule of mere earthen vessels, a limitation echoed in the Qur'ānic verse about intrinsic human weakness (Q. 30:54). Thus government faqihs, seduced by power, would dismay even dyed-in-the-wool stalwarts by the ease with which they add new, and not so subtle, inflections to the injustice of conjugation of the ill-omened verb 'to corrupt'. The twists of the turban may be politically more fraught than the religious sum of its folds.

It is a similar consideration that has led many other Muslims to question whether even under Islamic territoriality it is wise to employ force and coercion to propagate religion. One early caliph, for example, agonized over the safety of religious truth when upheld by the instruments of the state. This was the Caliph al-Ma'mūn, who declared in a public meeting in AD 830 that although under his rule many had converted to Islam for purely religious reasons, many others had done so from less honourable motives. 'They belong to a class who embrace Islam, not from any love for this our religion, but thinking thereby to gain access to my court, and share in the honour, wealth, and power of the

Realm; they have no inward persuasion of that which they outwardly profess.'[11] This anticipates Locke's notion of the jurisdiction of the 'outward and inward', and why territoriality offends conscience as much as it undercuts democratic pluralism, for if religion looks to political power for its ultimate defence, then it will find in that its sole vindication and reward, and, in time, its demise. We would, like the agonised caliph, be unable to determine the true from the spurious, sincerity from self-interest, or commitment from opportunism. Consequently, revealed law may not be domesticated into human schemes without direct risk to truth and the political scheme itself.

To look elsewhere for an example of the church–state distinction, in an instructive piece of debate between two Muslim scholars on the need for a theocratic state, we find identical issues being raised. One of the scholars in question, Muhammad al-Kanemī (d. 1838), the ruler of Kanem-Bornu in West Africa, challenged the *jihād* leader, 'Uthmān dan Fodio (d. 1817), with regard to the use of the sword for religious ends. Al-Kanemī said the sword is too rough-and-ready a weapon to use in settling religious questions, especially questions between Muslims themselves, since they would attempt to resolve by *force majeure* what might be substantial matters of theology, or even only differences of opinion. He insisted that Muslims must either settle for tolerance and mutual acceptance or else unleash a smouldering permanent war that would exempt, in his words, not even 'Egypt, Syria and all the cities of Islam . . . in which acts of immorality and disobedience without number have long been committed'. 'No age and country', al-Kanemī cautioned, 'is free from its share of heresy and sin.'[12] and any immutable division of the world between *dār al-Islām* and *dār al-harb* would fly in the face of this reality and reduce to ashes all sincere but inadequate attempts at truth and obedience. He could not find revealed truth in the blinding flames of fanaticism fed by short-fused fatwas.

There is a large body of material in both Christian and Muslim traditions, thus, to support a public role for religion without requiring theocratic rule. Sufyān Thaurī, a classical Muslim writer, has a witty aphorism apt on this point. He wrote, 'The best of the rulers is he who keeps company with men of [religious] learning, and the worst of the learned men is he who keeps the society of the king.'[13] That is to say, religion and worldly affairs prosper together when political rules are qualified by moral principles, and they suffer when moral principles are qualified by political expedience. In one pattern of political absolutization we elicit a contrasting pattern of religious relativization. So far as the moral foundations of human behaviour are concerned, church and state are, indeed, Hippocrates' twins: they share a common foundation in human affairs. Yet the one is destined for eternity and other for temporal ends. Ibn Khaldūn defends a similar position, though in his case he was stepping forward with the same distrusted secular foot twice. He wrote:

> The state whose law is based upon violence and superior force and giving full play to the irascible nature is tyranny and injustice and in the eyes of the law blameworthy, a judgment in which also political wisdom concurs. Further, the state whose law is based upon rational government and its principles, without the authority of the *Sharia*, is likewise blameworthy, since it is the product of speculation without the light of God . . . and the principles of rational government aim solely at worldly interests.[14]

In that statement Ibn Khaldūn describes and criticizes the Hobbesian state where political sovereignty is the basis of moral jurisdiction, with people's rights being what is secured to them by the national political sovereign.[15] Yet his alternative of a religious state creates the situation in which religion as a fundamental personal matter is placed under state prerogative. Ibn Khaldūn thus excoriates the power state only to reward it with jurisdiction over religion.

That argument John Locke took much further with his stringent critique of the Hobbesian state in his *A Letter Concerning Toleration* (1689), by stating that Christians as members of a 'voluntary society' were those who came together for 'the public worshipping of God in such a manner as they judge acceptable to Him, and effectual to the salvation of their souls'.[16] The overriding concerns of such a society, Locke felt, ought to be spiritual and moral, 'and nothing ought nor can be transacted in this society relating to the possession of civil and worldly goods'. Such a religious arrangement allowed for the triumph of personal faith.

However, between that conception of religion and of the state Locke drew a neat, if overly formal, distinction. He gave to civil government the responsibility for ordering our material well-being which includes 'life, liberty, health, and indolence of body', as well as 'possession of outward things, such as money, lands, houses, furniture, and the like'.[17] Just as the Church should not concern itself with the amassing of wealth and material possessions, so should government not concern itself with the salvation of souls.

This distinction between the nature of religion and of the state is not, however, satisfactory either in detail or in principle, as Locke recognized, for he went on to observe that government should not be given authority over religion because 'it appears not that God has ever given any such authority to one man over another as to compel anyone to his religion'.[18] For Locke, as for many Puritan divines, religion was incompatible with state enjoinment, not simply because the state is a pretty blunt and oppressive instrument to use in delicate matters of faith, but because 'though the rigor of laws and the force of penalties were capable to convince and change men's minds, yet would not that help at all to the salvation of their souls'.[19] That is just as true even if it is a democratic will.

Locke reasoned like that because theological issues were paramount for him in the following sense: a soul that was compelled was a soul that had lost its religious worth, so that it would not be a legitimate subject for spiritual regeneration. He asserted: 'true and saving religion consists in the inward persuasion of the mind, without which nothing can be acceptable to God. And such is the nature of the understanding, that it cannot be compelled to the belief of any thing by outward force.'[20] Similarly, the political commonwealth would be a tyranny if nothing beyond compulsion held it together. Such a religious conception of the moral integrity of the human person was necessary to Locke's conception of the tool-making character of civil government. Religion and civil government, Locke continued, have an overlapping legitimate interest in 'moral actions' that belong 'to the jurisdiction both of the outward and the inward court; both of the civil and domestic governor; I mean both of the magistrate and the conscience'.[21] In other words, religion as a voluntary society made possible the birth of the theory of limited state power. In this complementarity of church and state we find the 'good life' wherein 'lies the safety both of men's souls and of the commonwealth'.[22]

In the Lockean view, then, liberty is a principle of the people's God-given rights, rather than an indulgence granted by the sovereign national state. In that scheme, political rules may be effective without being sacred, and moral injunctions may produce practical fruit without being expedient. In neither case would people have to dance to the Vicar of Bray's tune in which the morality of taking the king's shilling is fixed at the king's bidding.

8

Caesar Crowned or Turbaned: The State as Pluralist Apparatus

The Muslim challenge and tradition examined in this brief account bring up the issue of how national secular state jurisdiction may find acceptance in the religious community. Muslims consider the *ummah* as a supranational community, one that transcends national identity. The reality, however, is that Muslims are not all assembled under one Islamic roof but are instead spread over many countries and subject to diverse and conflicting political jurisdictions. In virtually all cases, state authority has jurisdiction, however contested, over membership of the *ummah*, so that loyalty to the religious community would override, or else conflict with the claims of territorial sovereignty. Yet modernist Muslims, modifying the fundamentalists, would compromise with the national secular state by holding it to standards of justice and respect for human rights, or would otherwise settle for a benign liberal democracy with room for religious freedom. In its turn, the secular state, committed to toleration, would abjure the right to interfere with religion.

That liberal compromise commands wide support, bringing as it does religion into qualified association with the affairs of state, and making possible for church and state to be united on co-equality, instead of a mutually damaging adversarial relationship. Since religion stakes its reputation on moral commitment, the state cannot ignore it without risk of popular disaffection. For its turn, if religious doctrine is politically established, political differences would escalate into major theological schisms. If the state intervenes to suppress or enjoin appropriate forms of religion, that would infringe its own liberalism. It follows, then, that liberalism and religious freedom share one foundation, though church and state function as a split-level structure. Thus a way must be found for them to cooperate in society while restricting the state in its invasive power to encroach on conscience and religion from turning expedient and partisan, as expressed in some of the Muslim fundamentalist debate.

However, it is often the case that the secular state considers itself a competitor with religion for the moral ground, suggesting the state is not neutral. The Leviathan national state, whose inauguration the Abbé Sieyès trumpeted with such confidence, is in its nature girded for combat against all irrational forces, especially organized religion. The Muslim instinct to distrust it is, therefore, understandable. However, Muslim confidence should be tempered by the realities of the world, because even in places where *qāḍī* courts have operated, the Islamic code has not been free of its share of corruption and exploitation, and Muslims who have had cause to resort to them have not always found relief or justice. With the Sharī'ah becoming part of the political debate, Islam risks being reduced to a political enterprise in which the ultimate is turned into the expedient, and vice versa. Many Muslim modernists say such a course risks irreparable damage to the claims for revealed truth. Such modernists see a tolerant secular state as less threatening than a theocratic state. For, after all, there is plenty of scope in a tolerant secular state for exercising the duties called for by Islam's ethical system with regard to *Zakāt*, economic probity, education, domestic tranquillity, marriage, care for widows, orphans, the poor and the sick, rearing of children, good neighbourliness, honesty, forbearance, and so on. Modernists feel grievances in such matters are as much the consequence of internal failure and inadequacies as they may be of external infidel malice, and no amount of flaming *fatwa*s, or infidel quarantine, can immunize against so endemic an infection.

All religious systems are equally vulnerable to the relentless incursions of temporal compromise and to the vagaries of human instrumentality even, or especially, where human stewardship is claimed in the service of revealed truth. The Preface to The First Book of Common Prayer (1549), taking sombre stock of what had overtaken a religion trapped in human systems, expresses the sentiment well when it says, 'There was never any thing by the wit of man so well devised, or so sure established, which in continuance of time hath not been corrupted.' Herein is echoed 'Uthmān dan Fodio's own painful musing in his poem, '*Wallahi, Wallahi*', where he bemoaned the corruption that had riddled the theocratic reform programme he had initiated with the highest public ideals.[1] Religious truth cannot survive this corruption, for believers would become either cynics or Eliot's 'hollow men', a presence without consequence. The only reasonable answer is to separate church and state, to desacralize the political instrument while affirming religion's sacred calling.

These considerations prompt the following thought: separation of church and state need not deny the connection of ethics and politics, of church and society, of principle and precedent, or of faith and public order, a connection well described by Stackhouse as a 'buffer zone' between church and state, between piety and power.[2] For example, religious ethics may provide for the maintenance and security of the public order in such matters as family life, the socialization of children, interpersonal trust, philanthropy, compassion and humility without the public order being excluded from shared responsibility, though in that partnership public agents might be tempted to sequester religion as expedient leverage only, taking short-term advantage of revealed injunctions which are the source and spring of ethical life. All this indicates that modern arguments for distinguishing between public and private spheres would be hard to sustain on purely free-speech grounds, as Locke has cogently shown, for, however we define them, the private and public spheres are affected by identical rules of order, freedom and responsibility. State institutions would be expected to observe standards of freedom, justice, honesty, truth and decency no less than persons in community. In other words, the state in its nature distinguishes between right and wrong, punishes wrongful acts and offers incentives for right conduct. It is not morally neutral. Even in the intimate domain of family life, for instance, the rule of safeguarding and promoting the welfare of children is no less valid when transferred to the public realm than when it is viewed in its natural sphere of parental responsibility. Thus while separation defines the public and private domains, it does not abrogate the large area of partnership and overlap that turns out to be extremely fruitful of a humane and just society. There would be room in that partnership and overlap for absorbing Muslim ethical teachings and other values within an open, free and pluralist community.

In spite of such considerations, the debate as it has been conducted in many parts of the West has been a one-sided affair with Muslims taking the offensive and Christians reacting with calls for pluralism and multiculturalism, and with strategies of ecumenical unity striking for their ephemeral, tactical skittishness. If, by contrast, the example of Christendom and its disastrous consequences for genuine pluralism and multiculturalism were available to Muslims, it might calm passions and provide instructive lessons about the hazards of religious territoriality. Thus might the churches look for a state that is shorn of its anti-religious bias and is refocused on citizens' well-being and God's honour. Muslims need not then feel that the churches' rejection of theocratic rule is compounded of infidelity but in fact is inspired by sound religious doctrine.

International Muslim solidarity has aided and abetted national efforts, and has confused Christian attempts to respond to Muslim initiatives. Such is the case with the activities of the Organization of Islamic Countries (OIC) (*Munazzamah al-Mu'tamar al-Islāmī*) which was set up following the meeting of the Third Conference of Islamic Foreign Ministers, in March 1972. (Recent reports have also spoken of the creation of an Islamic economic bloc, called the Developing-8, or D-8, as a rival to the G-7 advanced industrial countries.) The first Secretary General of the OIC was Tunku Abdur Rahman, who resigned as Prime Minister of Malaysia to assume that position. The OIC was registered with the United Nations in February 1974. A number of Islamic agencies was established within the OIC whose religious character was spelled out in an official statement. This religious objective was described as the commitment 'to propagate Islam and acquaint the rest of the world with Islam, its issues and aspirations'.[3] The statement then went on to cite from the Declaration of the Third Islamic Summit of 1981, as follows:

> Strict adherence to Islam and Islamic principles and values, as a way of life, constitutes the highest protection for Muslims against the dangers which confront them. Islam is the only path which can lead them to strength, dignity and prosperity and a better future.[4]

The statement in that form and in its fuller version proposes a frankly utilitarian political view of religion, with the unsettling theological implication that Islam seeks for its adherents political and judicial instruments for their protection, and that only a temporary sacrifice need be involved in the process. Those who share in Islam's struggle, its *jihād*, will also share in its fruit, no more and no less. The problem with this reasoning is that it does not seem to work in reverse: many affluent and thriving communities, who are otherwise 'lodged in this world in a goodly lodging' (Q. 16:43), claim no scriptural credit for such advantage. By promising similar fruits to its adherents, religion, any religion, would be trafficking in double standards by placing the moral diacritic on political and economic goods but impugning those goods when their source is perceived to be the secular national state. If in the nature of the case the secular state or religion exists only to secure our material interest, that would make ends and means identical and make religion nothing more than a mere user-friendly tool. Thus, if both state and religion have as their common end the single goal of being 'lodged in this world in a goodly lodging', then the one would only be a duplicate of the other, and distinguishing between the two would defy even the most discerning. Religious pursuit and political interest would merge. We can avoid this situation only by drawing the distinction between church and state which was first inspired by Christian teaching and which allowed for the renewal and expansion of personal freedom and social responsibility in the West. Modern secularism was bred and weaned on Christianity, though it feeds on the fruits of Christian teaching to proclaim it has no appetite for the sources of that teaching. But the dragon will exhaust itself in eating its own tail.

The OIC statement, not to forget, ended by quoting the Qur'ān at 3:106, to the effect that Muslims 'are the best nation ever brought forth to men, bidding to honour, and forbidding dishonour, and believing in God' (Arberry). The phrase 'bidding to honour' is not sufficiently exact to reproduce the sense in the Arabic original of 'commanding the good and fitting',[5] a sense involving power and authority. 'The duty of commanding the good and forbidding the evil', Ibn Taymiyya insists as we saw, 'cannot be completely discharged without power and authority.' Member states of the OIC accept the binding authority of its charter, though the power and authority implied in the Qur'ānic verse it invokes might conflict with the sovereignty of national constitutions. At present the view has been expressed that the OIC lacks the power to hold member states accountable, even when it comes to the payment of dues. As it happens, this inadequacy in the structure of the OIC reduces its ability to challenge sovereign national states whose own internal domestic pluralism would make doctrinal conformity hazardous to enforce.

In terms of its historical origin, the OIC began as an organized Muslim response to the arson in August 1969, at the *Aqsā* mosque in Jerusalem under Israeli occupation, and in its original charter Jerusalem was designated as its *de jure* headquarters, with Jeddah being adopted *faute de mieux*. Before long, the activities of the OIC extended to numerous fields covering the social, political, economic, media, publishing, educational and intellectual activities. Membership in the organization was limited to sovereign nation states which are Muslim by definition, although several states with minority Muslim populations have joined, including Benin, Sierra Leone and Uganda. However, somewhat inconsistently, India and Lebanon, which have significant Muslim populations, have not been allowed to join. They have been disqualified by the territorial rule, for their heads of government by practice are non-Muslim. In 'territoriality' the religion of the ruler is the religion of the country, as we have remarked earlier. In other respects the OIC has applied stringent confessional criteria, from deciding on the venue of its meetings to granting economic assistance from its $2 billion development fund and awarding scholarships.

Although the OIC has agreed to work within the framework of the international security system in terms of explicit recognition of national state jurisdiction, it strives, in spite of that, to redirect the attention of member states to issues of international Muslim solidarity in terms of the primacy of the Sharī'ah and the unity of the *ummah*, i.e., code and community. Indeed, the religious counsels it has invoked for its *raison d'être* commit it to appeal to Muslims without regard to state protocol. For example, in its founding charter the OIC declared 'jihād [is] the duty of every Muslim, man or woman, ordained by the *sharī'ah* and glorious traditions of Islam,' and called 'upon all Muslims, living inside or outside Islamic countries, to discharge this duty by contributing each according to his capacity, in the cause of Allah Almighty, Islamic brotherhood, and righteousness'.[6] Such appeals reveal the OIC's distrust of secular national states even though publicly it says it respects and recognizes them. The ambivalence is also no doubt to be explained by the need to respond to Israel's dominance in the Middle East, as OIC's founding documents reveal.

Be that as it may, the OIC distinguishes itself from other international organizations such as the UN, the European Community, the Organization of African Unity (OAU), and even the Arab League by stressing its Qur'ānic identity as *ummah*. Yet the OIC as such has no independent sovereign power, and relies on member states to carry out its decisions. It has, nevertheless, identified the secular character of modern states as the consequence of Western intellectual hegemony and therefore as something that is in conflict with Qur'ānic norms and with the authentic Muslim aspirations they foster. By implication, Christian support or sponsorship of the secular national state is open to an identical objection.

Let us return to the issue of nationality as that form of political identity that in the secular West has primacy over religious identity, and say that the Muslim religious instinct is to oppose it as contrary to religion, more particularly to religion as public truth. National, ethnic or racial identity, founded on non-theist foundations, is in this view *shirk*, idolatry, for such identity divinizes natural and human traits, gives warrant to human self-sufficiency, whereas revealed truth transcends and relativizes the human scheme as such. Consequently, in spite of differences of culture and language, and in spite of a common desire to succeed economically, Muslims everywhere are, in the words of the legal manuals, 'bound together by the common tie of Islam that as between themselves there is no difference of country, and they may therefore be said to compose but one *dār* [i.e., *dār al-Islām*, "the abode of fraternal Islam"]. And, in like manner, all who are not [Muslims], being accounted as of one faith, when opposed to them [i.e., Muslims], however much they may differ from each other in religious belief, they also may be said to be one *dār* [i.e., *dār al-harb*, "the sphere of war and enmity"]. The whole world, therefore, or so much of it as is inhabited and subject to regular government, may thus be divided' along these lines.[7] This is the religious dialectic that sets out to distinguish between divine sovereignty and human inferiority, and yet produces the ironic effect of blurring the line between God and Caesar.

De Tocqueville called attention to this strand in the Muslim tradition, noting how the insistence of Muslims on the principle of a joint jurisdiction in church and state makes the religion a liability in an enlightened, pluralist democracy,[8] since faith and the public interest must under those circumstances coincide. Consequently, the pursuit by radical religious activists of Islam's comprehensive doctrine perpetuates the difficulty.[9]

Only a theological comprehension of this rigorous doctrinal position can be adequate to the many challenges it raises. The secular strategy of looking to assimilate Muslims into the Western mainstream actually evades the powerful effect religious territoriality still exercises on Muslims, even though important Westernized Muslim groups and individuals have tried to repudiate it. Religious toleration as understood in the secular scheme cannot in itself take care of the matter, since toleration is a weapon in the arsenal of secular attacks on the gospel.

Toleration must be reclaimed in its theocentric scope if it is to produce the fruits of the liberal consensus that is set to promote it. Without the Christian input, religious toleration will be empty. In reality, suppressing Christian religious practice by driving it into the sphere of pious intentions fashions the rod from which other religions will not be spared, unless, that is, like Islam they arrive in our midst through political channels which outwit the West's religious history. Thus in attempting to respond to the mounting claims of Muslims for a share in the public space, the secular champions of the public square have looked to legal and political measures without being able to recognize the religious source of those claims. And as long as any part of the Muslim territorial faith flourishes in one sector of our religious universe, it will feed the hope, however vain, of striving for its realization elsewhere. Mecca and Medina may be off-limits for the secular creed, but the secular world is not off-limits to their creed. If we say it is none of our business what happens in Mecca or Medina, intending that as a gesture of enlightened tolerance, we leave ourselves without safeguard for reciprocal consideration from Mecca and Medina. If they in turn say it is their business what happens in Manchester or Miami, we would have no answer, or at least no answer that is consistent with our premise of enlightened religious tolerance.

That is why religious toleration as a rider of modern agnosticism is in principle vulnerable to the Muslim push for religious territoriality, and any concessions based on that foundation would not foster interfaith confidence or trust but only a lopsided advantage. Consequently, the greatest challenge for the churches is not living with Muslims as such but overcoming the obstacles that the modern disaffection with Christianity has thrown up. The secular programme for religious pluralism has focused primarily on rescinding the claims of Christian uniqueness, a strategy that lowers the threshold for the religious uniqueness represented by other religions, and opens the way for Muslim radicalism.

The fact that such religious radicalism has grown and thrived in the West at a time when religious minorities established in religious territorial states have, if press reports are to be believed, continued to suffer civil disabilities shows how unbalanced the situation has become. As a prominent national political figure and TV commentator put it, playing somewhat to the gallery with a bait of his own, 'While Moslem minorities proliferate and prosper in Western societies that preach and practise freedom and tolerance, in nations where Moslems are the majority, Christians find the profession of the faith difficult, the preaching of the Gospel impossible.'[10]

The substance of that view, shorn of its crowd-baiting, is that a multifaith society as a split-level structure is ultimately untenable, with risks to democratic public institutions whose preservation depends on human rights being enshrined in religious life and practice.

Let us summarize the theological issue in religious toleration and in the separation of church and state with three points, viz.: (1) religious toleration is an essential part of human rights and, thus, of democratic pluralism; (2) it is necessary to separate church and state in order to protect human rights and to foster pluralism, and (3) the matter cannot rest there, because religious toleration requires arguments that go beyond those of public usefulness. Normative toleration as a safeguard of individual conscience is theological in the sense of being founded on the divine right of personhood, with implications for political liberalism. Now, while conscience, or the sanction for it, is not the business of the state, nevertheless, in its assumptions of moral agency, conscience touches inexhaustibly on the public order. Thus might religion produce fruits in projects of social welfare and their effects on public social ethics without religion turning into just pragmatic expedience, and thus, too, might state interest converge with religion without the state becoming a divine attribute. They complement each other when church and state are separated, but each corrupts – and is in turn corrupted – when the other co-opts it.

That consideration leads to the following conclusion: voluntary religious practice promotes ends that are constitutive of the values of a liberal democratic political community, though religion would be corrupted if it were co-opted merely as a tool of authority, and politics turn tyrannical if it ceased to be morally accountable. In this regard the temporal Islam of conservative Muslims, i.e., the claim for a public sphere for religion, may be reconciled with the ethical Islam of liberal Muslims without yielding to theocratic extremism on the right or to prescriptive atheism on the left. Thus we may concede the point of Ibn Taymiyya that 'the exercise of authority is a religious function' in the sense of accountability and subordination to the higher moral law, without granting that this requires establishing a theocratic order for the purpose. The political community is also the moral community, though the political and the moral, necessarily connected, are not identical. Truth is no less so even if it be politically inexpedient, while political expediency may serve the higher end without turning into the end itself. The political community, stretched to its extensive overlap with the moral law, cannot return to the exclusive dimensions of prescriptive atheism, so that, for example, when Ibn Khaldūn separates dogma and politics, truth and pragmatism, he expands the religious view while qualifying the political. Similarly, from the left we may agree with Locke when he argues for the 'outward' and 'inward' jurisdiction, with religion at the centre, without going so far as to say that separation removes religion from any role in the political economy. A theocratic state in Ibn Taymiyya's terms would be no better than an ideological secular state in John Locke's terms, for in both God and obedience to him would be reduced to tools of authority, with truth-seeking becoming a strategy for self-interest or group advantage, and vice versa. Separation of church and state, when taken to its logical extreme, would produce a doctrinaire secularism, aided and abetted by religious collusion; although without separation the situation may be reversed, yet identical consequences will follow, for then Caesar's political commissars will anoint themselves with the moral norms they confiscate from the Church. As such, separation does not mean exclusion, nor does it imply as alternative Hobson's choice of the state's absorption of the Church. It only means that religion is so important that the state should take it seriously, and yet is too much so for the state to expropriate it, and that although religion and politics are comprehended within the human scheme, religion exceeds the human measure by pointing beyond to the divine.

9

Conclusion: Political Realism and Theological Integrity

In view of growing signs of the pressure for temporal Islam, often expressed in terms of Sharīʿah and political power, and in view of the utter inadequacy of the sterile utilitarian ethic of the secular national state in meeting this challenge, Christians are faced with a question about supporting the pragmatist case for the secular state with moral principles. The state as the vehicle for tolerance, human rights, equality and justice must now be conceived in terms that are hospitable to claims for truth. Too much is at stake in the survival of the state as a non-corporate, non-doctrinaire institution to allow it to fall victim to our Enlightenment scruples about not mixing religion and politics. The pragmatist liberal scruple that proceeds upon religion in the fashion of individual entitlement and free speech is in one sense the spoilt fruit of the original insight about keeping Caesar and God separate, about ensuring religious freedom against state and power and jurisdiction. That insight become twisted into religion as individual entitlement and free speech, as a private rights issue under state jurisdiction, in fact as a matter of personal, individual choice without public merit. So Muslim critics are correct that rights without God are meaningless, but mistaken to suggest that a religious state would do better, because under such a state rights would spring from duress and intimidation, and that would scarcely qualify for freedom. If it is going to work, rights must presume an authority above and beyond individual or collective will, by general consent a transcendent tribunal that can support and adjudicate conflicting claims and interests. If we only have human authority as final arbiter of human rights, then there simply is no basis for saying one individual has rights of person and property against the multitude: against the individual, the multitude's will is irresistible and final by reason merely of numerical preponderance. Human rights as such is meaningless in that environment precisely because the individual has been assured no God-given rights. That is why human rights must presume a public tribunal insulated from the tyranny of numbers by being grounded in faith in the divine right of personhood, a faith that fosters the twin culture of rights and obligations, of freedom and community. In this context, state capture of religion is bound to dismantle the machinery of civil society, so that in one move of state divinization the brakes are removed from political excess and applied to freedom and commitment, in effect pressing political expediency into the service of a false absolute. All of that diminishes freedom and tolerance, two priceless and indispensable pieces of the apparatus of democratic liberalism.

In the nature of the case, democratic liberalism seeks political sovereignty from the people, rather than taking it to them, and so, to be successful, it rules and governs through consent. It is, therefore, a profound condition of its strength that religion flourish in it in the obvious sense of democratic liberalism using ethical methods in the pursuit of the public good. 'Despotism', de Tocqueville insisted, 'may be able to do without faith, but freedom cannot. Religion is much more needed in [an egalitarian democratic society] than [in a privileged, aristocratic society].'[1] It is when the ties of political control are relaxed that those of religion are tightened, when freedom expands that personal responsibility increases with it, and as men and women take control of their own affairs that they should be subject to the law of God. That much is clear on the political side of the equation.

On the religious front, it is when religion abandons territoriality that an inclusive territorial state can effectively emerge, and when religion demands territoriality that the state turns despotic. It is when people can enter into ultimate religious commitment, a commitment signifying the limitless possibility of human worth, that they are equipped to conceive a separate, limited domain of political action, so that the norms of moral truth can be distinguished from the tactics of political interest. Political sovereignty and state jurisdiction have their common foundation in the higher wisdom of the people's God-given rights, with religion the expression of that political axiom. Freedom is an act of faith.

Thomas Jefferson (1743–1826) appeals to this principle, invoking it as the last resort of democratic liberalism. 'I have no fear,' he affirms, 'but that the result of our experiment will be that men may be trusted to govern themselves without a master. Could the contrary of this be proved, I should conclude either there is no God or that he is a malevolent being.' Jefferson fervently supported separation of church and state not because he opposed religion, or his notion of it, but because he felt deeply that government would use religion to bolster its despotic powers. Religion was at its best, he argued, when it did not feel the necessity to compel compliance but remained an indispensable motive to moral conduct, and, he might have added in the same breath, democratic liberalism was at its soundest when it allied itself to religion's motive of freedom. That religious insight, allied to a faith that 'what is most perfect in government, in religion and in learning' still lies ahead rather than in a Gothic past, is fundamental to Jefferson's understanding of political power, and from it he could seek to put in place pragmatic structures of separation of powers with appropriate checks and balances among the executive, the legislative and the judicial branches of government. However, Jefferson sidesteps the issue of how truth and godliness may be maintained in the social and public sphere, a matter of singular interest to his New England Puritan forebears, especially Roger Williams, who distinguishes between the general magistracy of God's rule and the special magistracy of human authority.

John Dewey (1859–1952), with the same instinct for pragmatism, says similarly that those who are committed to democratic liberalism must 'face the issue of the moral ground of political institutions and the moral principles by which men acting together may attain freedom of individuals which will amount to fraternal associations with one another'.[2]

Christian teaching about God and Caesar thus constitutes the pillar upholding democratic liberalism, secured as it is on the consent of persons constrained by right rather than cowed by might. The state that can reach its people only through force will turn society into a battlefield, and the Church allied with such a state becomes moral coercion, making salvation a political prerogative. We would be ill-advised to abandon our faith in divinity on the basis of state fiat, or base it on the will of the collective, Rousseau's General Will with its unrealistic assumption about innate human goodness and reasonableness. Instead, we should see that the notion of peoplehood on which democratic liberalism depends itself hinges on the doctrine of persons 'born free, being the image and resemblance of God himself', as Milton expressed it, a view echoing the religious basis of peoplehood of classical Muslim thought, too.

The issue, then, has to be faced that the development of a democratic West was conceivable at all by virtue only of its Christian classical and Puritan developments, more specifically, by virtue of those marks, understandings, habits, disciplines, works and motives that belong with the teaching and influence of the gospel. How we spell out these marks of a Christian society is a task we must undertake as a collective responsibility. What is plain now is that society cannot be content with drawing on the reserves of Christian moral capital without attention to replenishing the source. Thus the presence of Muslims in our midst challenges us to begin some necessary stocktaking of where we came from and where we are headed.

At this stage we may redirect the Miltonian or Lockean view of religion and politics towards its modern day natural convergence with democratic liberalism in the following way. A liberal democratic state, however *laissez-faire*, must still impose laws and rules impartially on all citizens, and it is necessary to its success that such a state depend on a broad consensus concerning the fundamental constitutional axioms upon which laws and rules are based without a controversy about 'beliefs' in each round of rule-making. Thus disagreements may arise in society as to the material effects and consequences of rules, but not about the fundamental axioms and their source in religion and tradition. For example, the axiom, 'Thou shalt not kill,' as a scriptural injunction, would permit laws of murder to be promulgated and stipulated without the operative validity of those laws depending on prior assent to the authority of Scripture. Life is sacred because of divine affirmation, though the murderer or society need not affirm that to be subject to the law. In the law against suicide, for example, the point is poignantly made. Similarly, as a legal procedure administering the oath for the purpose of truth-discovery is valid even if the criminal would have no truck with confession and repentance as a religious duty. And without the assumption that the guilty may feel remorse, the judicial instrument will bounce back ineffectual. It matters supremely for the authority of law that human beings are deemed free moral agents and accountable for their actions, actions that can now be a legitimate subject of the law. It is the fact that these laws and rules may thus be detached from their source in religion and made impartially operative that gives them their force. Thus liberal democratic regimes are concerned with those procedural tasks deriving from a Miltonian or Lockean doctrine even if in substance those tasks do not require avowal of the religious source. You do not have to bring up the roots to know the tree is sound.

Political realism and theological integrity thus have a common purpose in distinguishing between a Caesar crowned and a Caesar turbaned, and that purpose is to prevent constituted government from meddling with doctrine. Politics as a self-sufficient comprehensive system of values concerned primarily with public order matters is already too well equipped to tempt it further with meddlesomeness in doctrine. In the power state, religion is addictive, for transcendence is fodder to triumphalist politics. Hence the caution that, although political liberalism can scarcely flourish without its foundational attachment in religious freedom, yet it will spoil from assuming primacy over the religious domain. If it knows anything to do with religion, the impulse of secular liberalism is to 'commodify' religion for value-added advantage, or, to amend de Tocqueville, government by habit prefers the useful to the moral and will, therefore, require the moral to be useful. By thus shortening the odds on the long-range, timeless truths of religion, the secular realm ends up removing the safety barrier against political absolutization and coming into conflict with George Herbert's religious rule that what 'God doth touch and own cannot for less be told'. Much of the church–state tension stems from the proximity of the two spheres, so that religion is too enmeshed in life not to profit, or suffer, from the state instrument, and vice versa, though marrying the two introduces an even greater risk of malignancy between them. Government with unlimited power will metastasize, leading to the adoption of injurious, despotic measures in the name of a prescriptive political code. At the same time, religion as a public-order strategy will become just a power game. Ultimately, whether the state repudiates or co-opts religion, it ends up feeding off religion: private piety as a liberal political concession is little different in restriction from the belligerent anti-religious stance preferred by the atheist state. We need the prophylaxis of separation thus to tame the state and to create a public space for religion without religious differences becoming a public liability. In the contemporary global situation, such qualified separation also provides crucial shield for pluralism and minority rights, enabling non-conformist groups and minority communities to play an assured role in the public sphere without fear of stigma.

Concerning the ultimate OIC case for the *ummah*, it may well be that, in principle, advocates of temporal Islam are right in their criticism of the national state as biased toward the secular metaphysic of the state as a moral idea, indicating that the secular state is not neutral towards the religious source of the moral idea, but is actively at work to supplant it for self-serving reasons. The suspicion is that the state wishes to establish the public sphere as a religion-free zone so as to designate it as a religious no-go area. Yet this stringent criticism is reserved also for the doctrinaire state, now dressed in purple velvet, yet whose religious metaphysic gives no immunity from despotism, since the religious state is still the captivity of dogma in the service of expediency. The actions of the religious state ultimately can be guaranteed to spare not even its religious sponsors, either as agents implementing harmful laws, or as the targets of such laws. That is why religion and government between them should be united in requiring the safety net of separation, a separation in terms of co-equal spheres of responsibility. Once we have secured that, then tolerance and pluralism can thrive, and with it religious freedom and political liberalism as fundamental issues of personal choice and freedom within a culture of justice and responsibility. All of which would ensure that minority status and religious claims could possess public merit without them carrying any stigma or reprisals, or the threat of any. Open and fair contest would determine for the most part, or for the part that matters, what survives or does not survive of the advocacy of ideas and values, and that ought to be the framework for a multifaith society.

Part Three

The Multicultural Myth

Jenny Taylor

10

Cultural Imperialism and the Bradford Riots

Introduction

Some Muslim scholars perceive the evil of a loss of religious faith in the West. They perceive the vacuum it leaves in every aspect of life, moral, political, intellectual and social. The Islamic discourse on our secular culture is penetrating and can be devastatingly righteous. Anti-secularists assert that the West robbed Muslim societies of their true essence through the colonialist onslaught and that this essence is now being restored by the Islamic 'awakening'.[1] There is a sense of pained indignation – and historic opportunity.

Seyyed Hossein Nasr, an Iranian Sufi now teaching in America who is highly regarded in Western intellectual circles, brings the point poignantly home. Before an eminent audience of academics and Muslim and Christian clerics, including the Bishop of London Rt Revd Richard Chartres at the inauguration of the new King Fahd Chair in Islamic Studies at London University,[2] he said: 'I don't think many western scholars really appreciate what is going on in students' minds in which all he holds sacred is desecrated and torn apart in the name of rational process or anthropology. It's a major psychological problem.'[3] He went on in the lecture to liken Western civilization to a 'cup' drained of religious faith. It still claimed global authority in the way the Christian 'paradigm' it replaced did before it. Yet it was a claim without legitimacy: a billion Muslims could hardly identify themselves with its basic irreligious premise. 'I don't believe in the global village. It was foisted on the Islamic world. That paradigm which replaced the Christian paradigm cannot be global. There is another reality out there that wants to claim for itself the pre-eminence of religion, because it challenges the predominance of secularism.' Describing the 'titanic battle' being waged by 'religion' against secularism, Christianity had met its match, he asserted. Islam, when not discriminated against, was the only alternative.

This sense of being the faith for the hour, to restore religious truth to a bogus empire, is empowering to some modern Muslims. Not only are they, along with Sikhs and Hindus, reconstructing their cultural and religious lives on British soil as a matter of course (and more completely than anything the anti-racist discourse, which concentrates on disadvantage, usually alludes to), but there is the added dimension of mission.

Missionary zeal partly accounts for the imaginative vigour with which Muslim lobbies are engaging with government in Britain across a whole range of issues, despite the crude political (and specifically south-Asian-political) sectarianism it often subsumes. Ethnic researchers point out that Muslims comprise two-thirds of the non-white members of the European Union. 'Islamophobia and the integration of Muslims will rightly emerge as key race-relations issues' notes Tariq Modood.[4] Ironically, they have used the secularity of the British system to achieve some of their ends. They have demanded and achieved concessions that are grounded upon their religious self-understanding – while the government has responded under the race agenda. But it is now possible to detect how the government is beginning to respond to Muslims as religious people too: the government in its regeneration policies is itself using religious motivation to drive through certain social objectives as we shall see, even though publicly the official view, that religion is irrelevant or private, has not changed. Indeed, the government's most recent Abstract of Statistics still classifies religion along with gambling among 'Leisure Activities'.

The following chapters look at some of the factors and challenges surrounding the presence of the religiously distinct Muslim minority in Britain and the anomalies in public policy being caused by a failure to recognize its distinctiveness at any deep level. In so doing, I hope to offer an incentive to Christians to reevaluate their peculiar vision and engage more boldly as religious people in public affairs.

I start with a discussion based on the Bradford Commission Report into the Bradford riots in 1995, when the frustrations of a particular ethnic community – in this case Kashmiri Muslim – burst upon the public consciousness. Why had the great panoply of social policy resulted in such anger among such a culturally distinct part of the population? Why had the well-intentioned anti-racist Labour politicians and others running Bradford – and the number of reports and the level of funding indicate nothing if not good intentions – been so wide of the mark? The contradictions and confusion evident in the details of the Report could mark, I believe, a watershed in how the government deals with this section of its ethnic minorities. Fear springs from ignorance – and the riots which sprang from the deep mutual ignorance that characterizes our so-called multiculturalism signal a new opportunity not just to understand and be more honest with each other as people groups, but to re-envision a future that must be inhabited together.

Working as a journalist, I dig out some of the writings and sayings of the experts about the anomalies in public policy and practice that characterize our society's muddle about race, religion and identity. The issues which have been surfacing in the journals and doctoral theses of academic lawyers, social anthropologists and political scientists over the past ten years convince me that there is far more need for a robust presentation of the gospel than the nervous sloganizing about values and anti-racism we tend to hear.

I also give an indication of the direction some Muslim scholars are taking their thinking, deriving from the anti-Western writings of Seyyid Maududi – which lends an urgency to the search for a common basis for our lives together in Britain. If faith is once again a political issue, forced onto national agendas and into legal precedent by religious people whom the government has previously thought it was dealing with on a relatively safe, secular agenda of racial justice, then we are witnessing a religious and intellectual change of deep significance. And if that is the case, Christians have got some hard thinking to do.

There are two things to add to this point. Islam is not a seamless whole, and Muslims in Britain vary in terms of adaptation to cultural influences, economic performance and educational attainment. The family's country of origin is a significant aspect of diversity, be it Middle Eastern, African Asian, Pakistani or Bangladeshi, as is well documented elsewhere. There are the urbanized exponents of 'High Islam' generally oriented in Ernest Gellner's definition 'towards puritanism and scripturalism', who tend to do business with Britain's elite. They shun many of the excesses exemplified by Low Islam with its saint-veneration and magic which 'knows literacy . . . mainly in the use of writing for magical purposes', i.e. amulets and spells.[5] High Islam moves and shakes the British Establishment and gets in the papers. Gellner believes that High (reformed or normative) Islam which has periodically lapsed into Low or Folk Islam, as expansionist zeal has given way to communal consolidation, is here to stay. It offers both a 'back to basics' form of the religion – Muhammad after all stands for monotheism cleansed of all mediation and superstitious association – and the chance of self-reformation suited to the pared-down requirements of the modern technological age. Plurality exists within Islam in Britain as much as within the culture at large: an important point in a democracy so often swayed merely by what gets into the media. Nonetheless there are distinguishable family likenesses which render discussion about 'Islam' and 'Muslims' valid without running the risk of stereotyping.

This brings me to my second point. Some of my initial comments appear to be negative. I have risked pinpointing a few of the recent more controversial aspects of 'Low' Islamic cultural practice only to make more clearly my point about the double standards multiculturalism seems to force people in positions of authority to take. Where inhuman cultural practice apparently sanctioned by a form of religion is tolerated by officialdom in the name of 'pluralism', we should grasp the nettle, without prejudice.

The Riots in Bradford

In early June 1995, a clumsy police arrest of jeering Asian street footballers sparked a weekend of rioting in the heart of Bradford. Frustrations and misery boiled over in the predominantly Azad

Kashmiri ward of Manningham – and spread into the city centre. Police reaction indicates, as observers testified, that police ignorance of and distance from their Asian charges was like fuel on burning tinder. They 'regarded the Asian community as aliens, and did not know how to handle them'.[6] The group of eight aggressive young Asians swelled to about 100, including women and children, as neighbours emerged to see what the noise was about. Rumour piled on rumour as to what actually had happened: police drove over a youth's foot, they attacked a baby in a woman's arms . . . Evidence was never produced in court of either incident, but it is clear that mutual mistrust and hostility was everywhere evident.

Precise details of what happened next are confused, and this is not the place to go into them fully. What is clear is that by 10.50 pm on the second night – Sunday – Bradford had become a battleground, culminating in a raid on the city centre, with plate glass windows being smashed, pubs attacked and shops looted. Young men in taxis and private hire cars followed, taking in the loot. Passing vehicles were attacked, their occupants and pedestrians threatened and intimidated. A local news photographer was threatened with death twice, his film torn from his camera at knife-point. Some estimates were of 700 youths on the rampage. Three hundred police officers were deployed to restore order.

The events were not considered significant enough for a judicial inquiry. Damage to 102 premises – all but four of them 'white-owned' – was estimated at around £0.5 million. Of 41 people arrested, only 16 were convicted of any offence and just one punished with imprisonment for robbery. In the words of Charles Forgan, Bradford Congress Secretary: 'The Government took the view – there have been enough riots; we understand riots.' Justification for such complacency is hard to find. Bradford Congress, a 'partnership' of eight public institutions including the local authority and the Chamber of Commerce, published its own report 18 months later in which it described 'the awful realities of life for many people in Bradford in the nineties and beyond'. It concluded: 'The alternative to reliance on increasingly inadequate public services at a time of reducing revenue support seems to be civic chaos.'

Reasons Given for the Riots

The 'official' causes of the riots in the Manningham area of Bradford, according to the Commission's research, were heavy-handed policing in a culturally 'sensitive' area, ripe for 'protest'. Britain's fastest-growing Asian settlement[7] had proved itself (to the press) to be just another cumulative victim of racism, youth unemployment and the deficiencies of the education system.[8]

A closer reading of the report, however, reveals a more complex and disturbing picture of a closed world, linguistically isolated because of its almost uniform practice of trans-continental marriage, and neglected by the wider society too hamstrung by actual racism – or just as frighteningly the fear of being accused of it – to come to its aid. This is the picture painted by Mohammed Taj, a local trade union leader and the third member of the three-strong Commission, who resigned in frustration at 'the report's lack of intellectual coherence and courage'. It was both soft on racism and insufficiently critical of the Muslim communities, he charged. 'The report utterly failed to address the real self-inflicted wounds that affect the Asian communities,' he wrote.[9] It blamed the city's institutions and then thrust the responsibility to problem-solve back at those same institutions. Police racism consolidated the problems, it is clear, and accusations of it spearhead his comments. Then he catalogues several other factors. Under the heading: 'The Asian Communities – Failings and Responsibilities' he lists:

1. Hostility to British culture: the term 'integration' has become a negative. 'Far too many members of those communities feel that being more comfortably integrated in British society necessarily means abandoning a distinctive culture and betraying their religion.'
2. Factionalism: 'The multiplicity of community, religious and cultural organisations prevents the communities having a coherent and forceful voice about their own most pressing interests. It is a besetting sin of leading community figures wanting to be "big fish in small ponds" rather than mere contributors to a more unified representation.'[10]
3. The Qur'ān school: 'Muslim communities hinder the educa-

tion and subsequent attainment of their offspring by imposing unfair burdens of extra curricular study at the Qur'ān school, mainly Arabic rote learning, not accompanied by guidance in an accessible language . . . leaving [them] tired and unresponsive to their wider education.'

4. Poor English competence: children are 'trapped in a language ghetto' created by the use of an Asian tongue as the sole domestic medium of exchange.
5. Muslim solidarity: an 'unwillingness to be self-critical'.

A picture emerges of a kind of mutual cultural 'stand-off' – despite thirty years of Asian settlement – and a nervousness or resistance to confronting the difficulties that the report repeatedly describes as ominous: the police use of a dog on people whose culture regards the animal as unclean; the anticipation of police mistreatment by older members of the community based on routine mistreatment in Kashmir. Something clearly should have been happening to break down the walls of prejudice. Ignorance can be detected everywhere, acting as a seedbed for hatred.

'Cultural Imperialism' and Clan Marriage

According to some estimates, by 2011, 27 per cent of the population of Bradford will be Pakistani.[11] Half live in what the report calls 'areas of stress', characterized by under-achievement in school, unemployment, poverty and overcrowding. Racial discrimination is one factor. The apparent maintenance of language deficiency as public policy is another. One upper-school headteacher told the Commission that rigorous English acquisition had been soft-pedalled. For example, over 80 per cent of the pupils in his school had been in the Bradford school system since they were five (or in many cases three) but teachers estimated that up to 50 per cent of them needed English language support. 'Such pupils are not peculiarly "dim" – they just have not been given an awareness that competence in standard English is crucially important for future life changes,' he told the Commission.

So, we have a sadly ironic situation whereby in a laudable attempt not to appear too Eurocentric, Bradford's educational

> policy planners may well have increased inequality of opportunity by not emphasising the centrality of effective English acquisition, which I firmly believe is the key to helping Asian families prosper in England . . . There have been years of collusion and mixed messages from the education service on this topic. (Para. 6.5.10)

The politics of multiculturalism saw the encouragement of English language learning as potentially threatening to immigrant family life. The report notes that: 'The values attached to one's mother tongue, and to the values of those on whom we depend as young children, cannot be over-emphasised as a basis for security.' This, it says, was the governing principle behind the LEA's approach. Yet such an approach, affecting the futures of people who came to Britain expressly to escape poverty (Para. 5.5.6) is questionable. 'Cultural imperialism' – a phrase that cropped up several times during the report's research – was considered an evil greater than social helplessness.

One Kashmiri parent is quoted as saying: 'Children starting in school still can't speak English. People like me should have been pointing it out. Our children are not White, and don't feel British. The identity of our children is the crux. Language is important for that.' And yet, three months before the riot, the government had announced its intention to withdraw extra funding for English language support in Bradford, under a total scaling-down of provision under Section 11 of the Local Government Act. According to Charles Forgan, the government mistakenly reckoned on language deficiency as a thing of the past: Pakistanis had now been in Britain for three generations.

Nothing could more symbolize the triumph of hope over reality. For, as a recent survey undertaken by the Methodist Church with NCH Action for Children shows, education will be increasingly important for the future welfare of Britain's cities. 'Over the next two decades, employers will place a higher premium on flexibility, solid educational attainment, computer literacy and good communication and social skills, even than they do today . . .'[12]

A further major factor in Bradford was trans-continental marriage. Until recently, nearly all marriages among Bradford's

Pakistanis were contracted abroad. Now the figure is 50 per cent – or around 600 a year.[13] Werner Menski, Reader in South Asian Law at the School of Oriental and African Studies, calls it 'the leaking tap of family reunion', and human rights provisos mean that no government can turn it off. In a paper that highlights the state's 'lack of honesty' on minority law, he writes: 'We witness desperate attempts by those in charge of the law to reassure the public that immigration can be controlled, but it is a fact that in this field . . . the law has definite limits.'[14]

Each marriage contracted in Pakistan was deepening the linguistic and cultural isolation of the Bradford ghetto – cousin marriage is the norm among Pakistani Kashmiris – while the government persisted in its belief that the need for top-up English language provision should have run its course. Philip Lewis, the Bishop of Bradford's Adviser on Interfaith Relations and author of an authoritative book called *Islamic Britain*, worries that: 'A section of the community is imploding because of clan marriage. Choices have consequences. If you choose these marriages there will be dire consequences. You are locking your community into a linguistic ghetto.' Many of the marriages, which are now the principal means of immigration into Britain, end in tragedy of a different kind. In 1996 in Bradford District alone, 178 girls of Asian name – 168 of them Muslim – ran away from home specifically to avoid arranged marriages. 'That's the tip of an iceberg: they're the ones the police locate in refuges or from referrals,' says Lewis.

West Yorkshire Police employs Britain's only Community Officer solely concerned with 'female Asian run-aways'. Philip Balmforth is based at Toller Lane Police Station in Bradford, where the riot had started two months before he took the job. His database has 630 names on it, built up since 1991. A retired former police inspector, he blames the government for women's suffering. 'The only way you can get people into the country legally now is through marriage. These rules are forcing these girls into all sorts of scenarios,' he says.

Philip Lewis says something similar: 'It will not do for the Muslim communities to keep on rubbishing the education system and blaming everyone else for their children's under-achievement. The worry is more and more kids are being locked into this. The issues are urgent and there needs to be a wider debate about it. It's no good saying it is illiberal saying these things. We are creating an inflammatory situation in this city.'[15]

We can conclude that trouble was inevitable with many Muslim households suspicious of British life and in some cases reluctant to seek to join it. Even where they wished to join it, they were *prevented* from doing so by key social policies. On the government side, confused aspirations at every level, combined with a 'reactive' immigration policy, left the volatile young to express the heartache of our muddled times.

11

Multiculturalism and the Cult of Silence

Multiculturalism or Racism?

Culture and religion are not the same thing, nor are they regarded as the same in law.[1] Yet religion informs culture, sanctioning much of its social practice whether consciously or by a kind of social osmosis. Peter Berger starts his famous book on the subject, *The Social Reality of Religion*, with the words 'Every human society is an enterprise of world-building. Religion occupies a distinctive place in this enterprise.'[2] Disentangling religious essentials from cultural accretions is perhaps an important challenge for future generations. Yet, for the time being, those entanglements form real issues for public policy. In this section I find it necessary to talk about culture and religion inclusively.

Bradford's problems embody an intellectual ideal that began as respect for culture and ended up as official indifference to real people. No-one was specifically to blame for Manningham's unhappiness, but certain factors over and above unemployment can be identified from which we must learn. Some of these were clearly to do with official nervousness about tackling problems perceived to arise from 'their culture'.

A perfect example of cultural inhumanity becoming ensnared by official cultural delicacy – taken from another city – was documented by a journalist investigating the case of Shazia Shafee, a 13-year-old Pakistani girl who disappeared from school in Sheffield for 20 months, and neither her teachers, nor social services nor the Foreign Office questioned her whereabouts.[3] Even if they had, there were few, if any, practicable sanctions available to them. After being beaten by her father evidently for becoming too Western – her parents had burnt her Western clothes – she was sent to Pakistan to 'teach her a lesson' and, barely pubescent, to be married to her cousin. *The Times* claimed she was 'placed into slavery'. In fact, Shazia was sent to live the life of an average young Kashmiri countrywoman. The reporter's shock at the conditions which are the common lot of much of the Third World is at odds with the bland disingenuousness of much British public comment on the multiculturalism it professes to celebrate.

> She lived in a hut with a variety of near and distant relatives, a single room where men slept on one side and women on the other. There was no sanitation: the fields doubled as lavatories and she could only wash after fetching water from a distant well. She was put to work: long, gruelling days of domestic labour. Later she would graduate to the even more arduous toil of cutting crops in the fields.

Shazia was eventually 'rescued', says the report, after smuggling desperate letters to the agony aunt of *Woman* magazine, who contacted a friend on the *News of the World* who fetched her, pursued, says the reporter, by a 'howling mob' of enraged villagers. She is now living with her English foster mum in Sheffield.

The reporter permits herself the luxury of indignation sanctioned by the 'victim's' voluntary adoption of status as an honorary 'one of us'. One minute she was 'a 13-year-old Sheffield girl who liked chips, clothes and *EastEnders*; the next she was a slave labourer in rural Pakistan'. Would the offence have caused such outrage if Shazia had kept her shalwar kameez and resisted the accoutrements of the West? Undoubtedly not. The West's prime value had been impugned: she had been refused the right to choose. Had she acquiesced not only in her own abuse, but in breaking the law on school attendance – as happens in thousands of largely unremarked cases in Britain – *The Times* would have had no story, because Shazia would have been ideologically 'black'.

The double standards are rife throughout public life. No-one followed up on Shazia. The Foreign Office is quoted in the piece as saying: 'You can't force ideas on people who have held different ideas for generations. You don't know who is on the right side, or even if there is a right side.' This is multiculturalism, in its stark post-modern form. The police and social services remained mum and, according to Southall Black Sisters, will remain so until public opinion becomes more coherent on the subject.

> [They] think it's a cultural practice, that it would be seen as 'intolerant' to do anything. We have even had to take social services departments to court to force them to have a girl taken into care. It's part of multicultural politics. They're frightened of the reaction they'd get from the families and the community – frightened of being called racist or being accused of interfering in minority cultures, of being called intolerant or oppressive.[4]

Nick Ralph at Sheffield Social Services Department is quoted as describing the problem as 'a clash between legality and religious ideologies'. British law on under-age sex has no jurisdiction in Pakistan. 'I don't think it would be right, because of the wider implications, to try to deculturalise an individual, to deliberately undermine her faith or the beliefs of her family.' His ideological position, which perhaps starts out as 'respect for culture', ends up as a form of racism. It is tantamount to a nation that spends millions each year tackling child abuse saying under-age sex has a different effect on Muslim girls than secular girls. And yet it is evidently no exaggeration to say that this kind of racism could kill. Hannana Siddiqui, Case Worker at Southall Black Sisters, is quoted as saying:

> [Girls] are sent in the first place often because the family feels they can't control them in this country. So they go to relatives where they are kept, or married, or both. A lot of the time they just submit and – yes – a lot of the time they are killed. There is a very high rate of domestic homicide on the Indian subcontinent; there are deaths among young women who have refused to cooperate. These 'honour killings' are a big issue.[5]

Siddiqui told me later that in this shocking paragraph two separate remarks were juxtaposed, and that she had thereby been misquoted. The truth was, if anything, worse. What she actually said was that there were girls who get taken back to Asia who were not heard of again. And the rate of suicide and killings around the honour of women on the Indian subcontinent was 'generally high'. What had not been researched is how many of the British girls who did not return could not – because they had been murdered.

Writing this is, as Mohammed Taj says, to risk comforting bigots while at the same time offending those within the Asian communities who are working hard to promote gender equality.[6] Yet it demonstrates that human rights exist only in the minds of those who believe in them. Personal autonomy – your presumed right to your own liberty – the basis of law and public policy for a generation, breaks down under the writ of 'multiculturalism', and silence reigns. Such a right protects the family from state interference, but affords little protection for women or children within a family governed by another value system. Such a right secures religious liberty, but permits religions to oppress their own minority members.[7]

Alain Finkielkraut, in his book *The Undoing of Thought*, shows how anthropology set out to critique the abstract formalism of the Enlightenment 'for the express purpose of effectively cementing respect for human persons'. But respect for difference degenerated into entrapment within homogeneous blocs, deprived of true access to democratic safeguards; apartheid being the obvious illustration. This in turn was countered by denial of real difference in a dragooned universalism that, as Nasr, quoted earlier, points out, is not universal at all.

Following 1947, the bureau of the American Anthropological Association submitted to the United Nations a project for a Declaration of the Rights of Man whose first article was redrafted as follows: 'The individual realizes his personality through his culture. Hence respect for individual differences entails a respect for cultural differences . . .'[8] Yet the achievement of this idea, when not tempered by other considerations, can be dehumanizing:

> At the same time in effect that we granted the 'other' man his culture, we robbed him of his liberty. He became nothing more than an interchangeable unit in a whole class of cultural beings.[9]

It has resulted in Britain in the toleration by British social workers of child marriage, polygamy and widespread educational absenteeism. Shazia is far from an isolated case. Kamran Shafi, minister of information at the Pakistan High Commission, describes it as 'a massive tragedy'.

Other Muslims (described as 'educated' in *The Times* piece) deny that such practices are Islamic, despite *hadith* (verified traditions) to the contrary that say that Muhammad himself married a child, Aisha, his second or possibly third wife. She was six or seven at the time of the betrothal – and nine when the marriage was consummated.[10] Muhammad is popularly conceived as the model for Muslim behaviour. In Low Islam, Muhammad's practice sanctions all practice, and therefore makes religious the practice of some British people which mainstream society finds distasteful. al-Ghazali says:

> God has said: 'Say: if you love God, follow me, and God will love you' (Sura 3.29), and He has said: 'What the messenger has brought – accept it, and what he has prohibited – refrain from it!' (Sura 59:7). That means, you have to sit while putting on trousers, and to stand when winding a turban, and to begin with the right foot when putting on shoes.[11]

To mention this in the context of Shazia Shafee is no cheap shot. Cities like Bradford and cases like Shazia's will continue to be a focus of tension because our inadequate version of multiculturalism can lock individuals into a situation neither they nor the wider society would desire for themselves.

Multiculturalism a 'Cult of Silence'

The crisis for policy-makers will deepen, if only because even now many in key positions are refusing to admit there is a crisis. The Bradford Commission called it a 'cult of silence' and identified many examples of issues being avoided.

> *On language teaching*: 'It is clear to us that puzzlement at the lack of priority given to tackling this problem is very strongly, and very widely, held . . . clear leadership is urgently needed. It is vital that explicit political discussion and prioritisation

of this challenge should be undertaken *urgently*' [my italics] (Para. 6.5.18).

On domestic abuse and violence (only very recently recognized as criminal in Britain): a general cult of silence which prevailed about such matters (Para. 5.38.4).

On hooliganism: 'In public places, White adults hesitate to intervene where Asian children or youths are concerned, in case they are accused of being "racist", a not uncommon response' (Para. 5.24.2).

On race relations policy: '. . . the heat generated by the Honeyford Affair caused many White people to avoid discussing openly what might be racially sensitive issues' (Para. 5.15.5).

On local politics: '. . . failure to open up to constructive discussion issues which are thought to be controversial . . .' (Para. 2.10.1).

On demographics and the exploding population: '. . . these dangers are known to the council's demographic researchers, but fears of racist reactions in particular lead to caution in discussing and publicizing data'.

This cult of silence, far from protecting minorities from discrimination by the wider society, has led not just to an inability to target resources accurately, but more seriously, as was evidenced by police action in Bradford, to almost total cultural separatism – in fact, informal apartheid. Neglect would appear to have been government policy. Werner Menski has written that

> during a recent conference on the role of research about minority communities in Britain some participants held their breath when told by a government official that 'there are certain things we do not want to know'. This was as clear a statement as one could get of official avoidance policies towards ethnic minority issues in Britain.[12]

Menski describes this as 'purposive non-discourse' – a glorious expression for burying your head in the sand.

12

Religion, Law and Social Policy: The Myth of Neutrality

Multiculturalism and the Law

It is in the law that the deep-seated nature of our 'culture-muddle' is beginning to be manifest. The secularization thesis which denied real significance to religion, also suppressed intellectual life. By divesting religious actors and institutions of their social, economic and political influence, it at the same time permitted anomalies to flourish in many disciplines and a downgrading, or 'disenvisioning', of public life. Only now is it becoming respectable again, for example, to write about the deep interrelation of religion and law.[1] It is only the presence of minorities with different legal systems based in holy texts that has allowed this particular debate to resurface. For such minorities the privatization of religion is unthinkable. Yet the English legal establishment has resolutely maintained the secular fallacy that it is 'neutral on religion'. This was most clearly expressed by Lord Justice Scrutton in 1961, in the case of Re Carroll – 'It is, I hope, unnecessary to say that the Court is perfectly impartial in matters of religion' – and Cross J's comment in Neville Estates Ltd v. Madden: '[a]s between different religions the law stands neutral'.[2]

If the law regards itself as 'religion-blind', despite the significant role religion plays in shaping cultures and societies, it follows that there is no proper public policy on immigration, integration and citizenship, as is in fact the case. There is merely a reactionary approach based on numbers and place of origin.[3] The Home Office itself, as long ago as 1971, was saying:

> Immigration law in this country has developed mainly as a series of responses to, and attempts to regulate, particular pressures rather than as a positive means of achieving preconceived social or economic aims.[4]

Government policies have developed as knee-jerk responses to the perceived crises caused by successive waves, first of migration from the New Commonwealth and latterly of asylum-seekers. The left-wing Institute of Public Policy Research (IPPR) offers in its stead a policy based on economic indicators, 'rather than purely humanitarian considerations alone'. Britain's prosperity should alone furnish the yardstick of its hospitality, it believes.

The IPPR gives up altogether on the question of citizenship.

> There is a duty to be law abiding, but to what extent is there a duty to obey norms that are not prescribed by law? Must all good citizens speak English? Must all good citizens keep to monogamous relationships? Defining the duties of citizenship can be exceedingly difficult in a multicultural society. Perhaps it would be neither possible nor desirable to attempt such a comprehensive description.[5]

The magisterial impartiality of the state in religious and hence cultural affairs, in which light Lord Justice Scrutton saw himself, is anachronistic. It is a throwback to a Christian age that established tolerance as the proper attitude to matters of private religious observance, when there was no radical challenge.[6] Yet, the law has not kept pace with religious pluralism caused by immigration.

Research by Anthony Bradney has shown that the law is neither neutral nor coherent, yet, in a climate of purposive non-discourse, as Menski has argued, there is little basis left for discussing that fact.

Most people will be aware of the exemption Sikhs won in 1979 from wearing crash helmets on motorcycles. Fewer will know of a more subtle, but just as significant exemption, which privileges religious muscle. In 1989, Sikhs were granted exemption from laws requiring the wearing of safety helmets on construction sites under the Employment Act, which was not extended to Rastafarians, despite various biblical injunctions such as Leviticus 21.5, observed by Rastafarians, that require that hair should not be cut. Lord Strathclyde, who argued the government's case, resisted extending the exemption to other areas of work and, implicitly, to other religious groups, but was clearly swayed by the weight of political pressure in his reasoning. There was, he argued, 'no similar concentration of Sikhs in any other industry' and implicitly, there was no similar concentration of any other relevant religion in the construction industry.[7] Bradney won his doctorate for demonstrating that the law is not neutral as regards religion, if it forces a religious group to choose between employment in the construction industry and the dictates of their faith. In other words, Sikhs mobilized more effectively than Rastafarians. Religious 'neutrality' as observed by the state is in fact a numbers game.[8]

Similarly the Shops Act of 1950 made allowance for Jewish religious observance – allowing them to open for trade for half the day on Sundays – but made none for Muslims. In other words, the law treats as less important the holy days of some religions than others. This is not neutrality, and to regard it as such is dishonest, confusing and, paradoxically, divisive.

At a recent public lecture, Werner Menski told his largely Muslim audience: 'People react by strengthening their legal allegiance', i.e. to the Sharī'ah.[9]

Again, Jews won special treatment under the 1976 Race Relations Act as both a racial and a religious group. In Seide v. Gillette Industries, an Employment Appeal Tribunal decided that 'Jewish' could indicate either a racial or a religious group for the purposes of the Act. This is a privilege which Muslims, who also see themselves as racially and religiously distinct, are denied, and which they regard as discriminatory, despite the fact that Islam does not consider itself limited to a particular race and accepts at least two distinct theological denominations and several legal ones.

The Act outlaws discrimination on the grounds of 'colour, race, nationality or ethnic or national origins'. In 1983, during the Appeal of Mandla v. Dowell Lee, which went to the House of Lords, Lord Fraser argued that 'ethnic' did not have a strictly racial or biological sense, but could be defined as 'a community by virtue of certain characteristics'. Of these, two were essential: first, a long shared history; and second, 'a cultural tradition of its own . . . often . . . associated with religious observance'. Five other criteria were not essential but could be relevant, one of these being a common religion 'different from neighbouring groups or the general community surrounding [the group in question]'.[10]

Thus this case, which defined 'ethnic group' as a legal category for the first time, cleared the way for religious territoriality to become the basis for securing concessions from the majority population. In other words, a religious ghetto like Manningham with all its woe, is regarded as an entity in law, with extra rights.

The 1976 Race Relations Act can be used therefore both as a basis for discrimination between ethnic groups themselves (Jews and Sikhs[11] over against Rastafarians and Muslims – the latter because they are regarded as having diverse histories and cultures and are religiously fissive). And it can be used as a force against integration, towards increased territorial consolidation. On neither count is the law neutral towards religion – and both bode ill for wider social cohesion. Given the confusion of the law as to its own neutrality, and the failure of government openly to discuss it, minorities are establishing their own rules. The total absence of debate about what religious underpinnings the law really has, and about what kind of Britain most people want, has permitted minority groups, as we shall see, to pursue their own separatist agendas.

The relatively small percentage of people of 'Asian' background – reckoned to be 3 per cent (half of Britain's ethnic minority population, excluding students, refugees and illegal entrants) and likely to double by the end of the next decade – would not ordinarily pose a problem for legislators and service-providers. But the nature of settlement does. Asians are not thinly spread, but live mostly in concentrated communities (no longer exclusively 'inner-city' areas). Anthropologists like Roger Ballard call them 'colonies'. And these colonies have been reconstructing mental and even physical patterns of South-Asian social and religious life. What is more, plural religious legal systems have been able to establish themselves by default. The very lack of discussion and the law's inadequate understanding of itself, has actually caused the visible emergence of British South-Asian patterns of law in the UK. Menski writes:

> because of avoidance reactions on both sides, there has been an absence of discussion, a silent and more or less defiant dissent from 'the other'. Having declared itself superior, English law, with few exceptions, now refuses to negotiate change and modifications from its basic position of official strength and legitimacy, while the adjustment strategies of ethnic minorities are increasingly marked by avoidance reactions in the form of quiet 'inner migration'. This avoids outright conflicts and, thus, an open resolution of many of the issues that arise . . . religion remains a major factor in this context of purposive non-discourse.[12]

Ballard confirms this:

> Current research confirms that virtually all ethnic minority communities in Britain operate a pattern of resistance towards legal assimilation. Such patterns are closely linked to religious issues and seem to be most easily observable in the field of family laws.[13]

A case in point is 'limping marriages' that result from the practice of Islamic polygamy, which is followed in Britain (and has reached alarming proportions in the United States). A woman may obtain a divorce from the state but be denied one by her husband under Sharī'ah law. The man can, and frequently does, marry again under Muslim rules on polygamy, but the woman cannot. She faces rejection by her own community, and subsequent destitution – a catastrophe if the woman in question cannot speak English and engage with the wider society.

Halāl provision in schools and prisons (which subsequently provide *halāl* food for all pupils or inmates to minimize administrative burdens) is a well documented and relatively minor example of religion dictating public life – against the prevailing law. 'The law stipulates that the slaughtering of animals in accordance with the precepts of Islam is only permitted if performed by a Muslim for the food of Muslims.'[14] I know one primary school with a majority of Muslim children in Newcastle where all the meat bought in is *halāl*. There are bound to be others.

More significant for the purposes of this book perhaps is the hybrid system of obligations in Asian communities – *angrezi Sharī'ah*, as Menski has dubbed it in relation to Muslims – which consists of an 'intricate combination of the formal rules of English law and of the socio-religious rule systems of their respective communities'. Menski gives the example of a Muslim woman in 1990 successfully suing her former husband who had accused her of not being a virgin on their wedding night. She was awarded £20,000 damages in recognition of the slur on her and her family, 'bearing in mind the values of her community'.[15]

As Asians learn to adapt their own laws to mainstream law, so mainstream law adapts arbitrarily to the fact of other religious requirements. Yusuf Islam (alias former pop singer Cat Stevens), among others, escaped prosecution for incitement to murder when, on a BBC TV talkshow, he called for the fatwa against Rushdie to be implemented.[16] Yet there is some evidence to show that this plural value system, well-meaning enough, can be counter-productive and demeaning when it springs not from a clear sense that people are made in the image of God but from the confusion, cowardice and indifference that multiculturalism can disguise. In Bradford

> one particularly incensed Asian woman probably spoke for a lot of people in her scathing contempt for those Whites who excused, or failed to condemn, wrongdoing when the culprits were not White. It was, she rightly said, patronising, as well as stupid.[17]

Multiculturalism and Social Provision

Culture-blind immigration policies have prevented service-providers and the Church from entering into informed debate about the religious nature of human personality and its social implications. And yet the challenge the nation faces on this front is immense. The social order under the impact of immigration has changed more profoundly than at any time since the Norman Conquest – at least that is the view expressed by one anthropologist in a recent university textbook.[18]

Many of the new British suffer from the religious ignorance

wrought by the secular assumptions of wider society at every conceivable level. In healthcare and social work, the impasse between service and client is profound and serious. Hannana Siddiqui at Southall Black Sisters believes social services, police and others are 'failing in their duties to Asian women', for example by not checking up on absence from school – called 'holidays', but which may in fact be abduction.

Cultural relativism can cause inertia and injustice, and workable guidelines through the maze need to be adopted that uphold the truth and prevent suffering. The Christian model can be surprisingly straightforward. Midwife Alison Cottam, who works in a Midlands hospital with a large multi-ethnic catchment and who is also an evangelical Christian, found herself risking her professional reputation to affirm Asian patients in various cultural practices that ease pain but would be dismissed as 'silly' by her seniors. She cites the woman who has a bowl of water with a piece of something that looks like dried seaweed in it. 'This is Miriam's Flower,' the patient explains. 'It comes from Mecca, our holy city. The plant rehydrates in the water. As it opens up, so my womb will open up and the baby will be born easily. It always works . . .'[19] Cottam took the risk of hiding the flower, instead of throwing it out as would have been expected, because it was important to her patient. She observes: 'There's a kind of lip service paid to spiritual things – student assessment forms mention it. Yet most white people are not aware of their own spirituality or the religious side of things and it's very very marked and can cause real distress.'

Anthropologist Roger Ballard, at the Department of Religion at Manchester University, has written that

> marginalisation . . . arises not so much from discrimination, but rather from professional practitioners' inability to deliver, *even if they wanted to*, an effective service to their minority clientele, above all because they lack the requisite skills and sensitivities which would allow them to do so (author's italics).[20]

There is some evidence of response to this: the King's Fund, the London-based health research trust, established a new dedicated research unit, the Afiya Trust, as recently as June 1997. Yet a key text for practitioners in mental health published in 1995, *Mental Health in a Multi-ethnic Society: A Multi-disciplinary Handbook*, has no reference to religion or beliefs in its index, despite its dedication to 'all those who meet racism or cultural intolerance in the field of mental health'.

By and large, materialism still dominates public discourse and policy. The language of non-positivist truth, even 'beliefs', is still missing. Ballard for example, in the 1996 seminar paper from which I have quoted above, was having to exhort his colleagues in sociology departments to 'conceptualize the Asian mindset', i.e. to give intellectual assent to the need for models of provision that include other realities. A recent article bore this out.

> Public-health professionals appear to view knowledge and beliefs as contrasting terms. Knowledge refers to people's 'knowing' about modern biomedical information, such as the . . . importance of good nutrition . . . The term knowledge contains the implicit assumption that the information is 'scientific fact,' based on universal, cross-culturally valid 'truths'. The term beliefs, in contrast, usually refers to traditional ideas or 'folk models' . . . The belief systems of health professionals are supported by substantial empirical evidence, but they are beliefs all the same.[21]

This 'knowledge' bias has seriously distorted, even impeded, public policy. Yet, ironically, it was considered 'thoroughly alarmist', even racist, in liberal circles to consider the possibility that immigration would mean changes.[22] The false and limiting dualism of the anti-racist discourse has proved inadequate for social reality.

> Indeed this anti-racist perspective has now become so well entrenched in the social work, social policy and sociology literature that ethnographic accounts of the internal characteristics of minority communities receive no serious consideration at all.[23]

While noting that 'far from being helpless victims of racism, [minorities] always and everywhere demonstrate enormous powers of agency . . . the minorities have their own agendas', Ballard adds that 'any approach which fails seriously to present the richness of unfamiliar religious cultural traditions, and above all to challenge the deep-rooted ethnocentric presuppositions which are such a key component in the maintenance of racial and ethnic hegemony, are of little or no utility'. This poses an enormous problem for service-providers and sociologists, who tended to assume that religion was at best a retrograde symptom of a pre-industrial mindset and, at worst, a means of capitalist and racist subjugation. Philip Lewis makes the point that before the *Satanic Verses* controversy in 1989, the religious dimension of the settlers' personal lives was almost totally ignored by academics.[24] Ballard concludes that while modern 'religious studies' have been safely confined to the study of texts – the rubric – this is likely to change as the social impact of religion becomes increasingly apparent.[25]

Ballard's ground-breaking paper was presented, significantly at a conference held under the auspices of the Comparative Study of Religion. 'The issues simply do not rate high enough on the agendas of other equally relevant disiplines, and most particularly in Sociology and Social Anthropology, for such an enterprise even to be thinkable,' he wrote. A state of affairs which, he concludes, amounts to racism.

> If racism consists of a refusal to respect the humanity of non-European people seriously, such that the physical, social, cultural, religious and linguistic dimensions of their very being is comprehensively disparaged, there is only one epithet which can be applied to this state of affairs.[26]

In other words, academics who long ago jettisoned religious categories as a means of understanding anything will have to go fishing over the side of their boats to retrieve the unthinkable. Religion is once again become a live, as opposed to a merely textual issue – in public life, in law, in social policy, and in the academy – and any political vision for Britain, merely by the exigencies of existing race legislation, will have to take religion seriously.

If religion is once more a vital political issue – thanks in large measure, as we shall see, to the presence of Muslims in Europe – it presents an urgent opportunity for the Church both intellectually and practically to retrieve its sense of itself and its role.

State-aided Cultural Isolation

The consolidation of Asian colonies in Britain, from which there is at least only limited right of exit,[27] has been largely state-sponsored. Pnina Werbner has done considerable research into the phenomenon. Case studies in Manchester reveal 'a basic thrust to develop and elaborate British Pakistanis' cultural uniqueness', a point argued by other scholars, notably Dahya and Breton.[28] It goes beyond features common to all emigrant groups, such as specialized food shops and restaurants, places of worship, visiting artists and local cultural societies: religious observance is well catered-for in 'tolerant' Britain, allowing an expansive sense of generosity and patronage. 'The institutional completeness achieved by Asian immigrants to Britain is . . . quite remarkable; indeed, it is on a scale hitherto achieved only by European colonial settlers in the developing world.'[29]

Werbner makes the case that this thrust has been enabled both by state support and by local authorities.

> Local authorities provide libraries of South Asian imported books in Urdu and Punjabi as well as Urdu or Punjabi language classes or courses, while multi-cultural education units produce specialised 'ethnic' materials for schools. The Arts Council and Cultural Services fund minority art activities and multi-cultural festivals. The Manpower Services Commission and DHSS fund welfare and communal activities, together with the local Social Services. There are in addition, special radio and television programmes, for minority listeners and viewers. Indeed, the expansion of specialised services for minority groups appears to have taken on a momentum of its own, with important longterm implications . . .[30]

Werbner then makes the important point that 'many British Pakistanis see their religion not only as a source of all true values and morality, but as their only real protection from racism and racial abuse. A perceived attack on these values thus threatens to undermine the group's self-respect and ultimate shield from racial stigmatisation.'[31]

Werbner implies that maintaining a sense of religious difference is essential for survival. This together with the thrust for separate schools, the multiplication and perpetuation of state-funded voluntary welfare services and state-supported community centres 'is a trend which defines with increasing sharpness the cultural-cum-organisational boundaries of the ethnic community.'[32]

The maintenance of this sense of its own difference, ironically funded by the state, is at odds with the state's own public pronouncements, notably Douglas Hurd's speech to a gathering of Muslims following Ayatollah Khomeini's fatwa against Salman Rushdie in 1989. Speaking then as Home Secretary, he emphasized the importance of 'proper integration for ethnic minorities'. It is not clear whether he meant integration, or assimilation, as his Minister of State, John Patten, clearly did. In a mimeograph called 'On Being British', he urged 'cultural minority communities' to aspire to 'a norm'. That norm is characterized by 'those things which . . . we have in common. Our democracy and our laws, the English language, and the history that has shaped modern Britain.' At the centre of this history is the idea of freedom: 'freedom to choose one's faith, to choose one's political allegiance, to speak and write freely, to meet, argue and demonstrate, and to play a part in shaping events'.[33]

There is clear need for a vision of integration that does not threaten people's need to develop in their own way. The suspicion of a dragooned assimilation will always exist until a more creative consensus emerges on what society should aim for. Religion is inevitably part of that process, and it is increasing in significance by default – and by design. Its co-option as a political instrument is perceivable in the creation in 1992 of a new government department, chaired formerly by the Under Secretary of State at the Department of the Environment and now by the 'Minister for Regeneration'.[34] The Inner Cities Religious Council (ICRC) is part of an unprecedented process to harness faith groups behind government policies on regeneration; and until very recently, and after some persistence, it was inaccessible to public scrutiny. Journalists were neither invited to its regional meetings, nor permitted to interview its personnel. With a budget of £100,000, it makes a small but significant vehicle of religious allegiance to effect economic growth.

The brainchild of the then Minister at the Department of Trade and Industry, Robert Key, who raised the idea at a fringe meeting of General Synod in 1991 under the Archbishop of Canterbury, George Carey,[35] the aim of ICRC is to 'develop dialogue between the principal inner-city faith communities and Government, to foster partnerships in urban regeneration'. It received the seal of approval of Prime Minister Tony Blair at its relaunch in July 1997.

> I share your commitment to this venture born out of Faith in the City and the current Archbishop of Canterbury's determination to join in dialogue with leaders of the great religious faiths to address the problems of the inner cities and forgotten outer estates . . . You bring a broad perspective and a unique insight into these and other issues *to which we in Government are determined to listen*' (my italics).

The ICRC holds four Regional Conferences a year, attended by local 'faith leaders', and produces a Newsletter with a multi-faith orientation. Its Secretary is Anglican clergyman, David Randolph-Horn, a likeable, bearded enthusiast whose stipend is paid by Synod's Board of Finance (originally from the Archbishop of Canterbury's Discretionary Fund and bits of money from the various Christian denominations) and whose secretariat is funded by the DOE. It is part of the much bigger Single Regeneration Budget, established in 1994, and including City Challenge, Urban Development Corporations and Estate Action, which since 1990 has spent more than £12 billion on Britain's inner cities – funding specifically identified by Werbner as the means by which ethnic communities have sometimes 'hardened their cultural boundaries'.

Randolph-Horn relishes the direct access he has to ministers and is fairly universally trusted and even confided in. His post is non-denominational: it could be held by a Buddhist or presumably a Jehovah's Witness with the appropriate skills – chief of which seems to be diplomacy – and a willingness to sign the Official Secrets Act. The philosophy of the ICRC, in the words of its former Tory Chairman, Sir Paul Beresford, is 'to give local people the normal freedom and opportunity to maximise their opportunities'. He said, in an interview with the author:

> The Government's view is that regeneration needs to be holistic and there needs to be a combination for a community to be able to get to a point of life within itself, where the local economy takes on a new lease of life . . .
>
> Having come here twenty something years ago from a society [New Zealand] where there were virtually no poor people, virtually no rich people, where there was equality, opportunity, choice, I was quite shocked when I came here. I went and worked in the East End of London and I was appalled at the conditions people were having to live in and work in. But more than that, I was appalled at the difficulty to get out. And use the innate abilities that people have, be it intelligence, be it particular skills, be it just the freedom to choose.[36]

A walk around Elswick Ward in Newcastle, an inner-city multicultural 'community',[37] is instructive in light of these musings. Elswick is the poorest parish in the Newcastle diocese, rating 17 on the Church Urban Fund deprivation indicators. The qualifying rate for funding is 8. Over the past seven years, it has been the subject of various high-spend regeneration grants, part of Sir Paul's purse.

Much of the money has been spent on cosmetic 'landscaping' projects that deteriorate in weeks under the onslaught of trash and dogs and vandals. Community workers admit it's a magnet for crooks from other parts of the city, using unoccupied houses as a stash for stolen goods, or as drug markets. Terrible things happen with a kind of numbing monotony – largely because people know they'll mostly get away with it. The only manifest sense of ownership or identification with the place is pathological. A missionary who works there was assaulted in her own home in 1996 by white intruders, because, it is believed, they thought she harboured black lodgers. No-one truly feels they belong, so no-one cares. Litter catches at your feet as you walk the windswept streets. Many homes in the red-brick terraces are boarded up, gutted by fire. What would it have been like without the expenditure?

Any casual observer can see the resistance of some communities to 'regeneration'. Either Sir Paul's idea of 'holistic' is not whole enough – as is so evident in other areas of public policy – or it's been ignored. The latter likelihood is borne out by *The Cities*, a report produced in 1997 by the Methodist Church with NCH Action for Children. The writers assert that in effect the Scarman Report's recommendations after the Brixton Riots in 1985 were not implemented. Instead of concentrating on 'holistic' regeneration as he suggested, they threw money at improving the look of things. Clearly it's easier to plant a few trees, and pedestrianize a precinct, as missionaries know, than to get at what's really bugging people. It raises the obvious and profound question, Can a secular society ever meet its objectives if it discounts what makes people human: the soul? In fact, all materialism can do is work on the material: '[f]or much of the 1980s,' the NCH report goes on, 'urban policy was moving away from these [holistic] values, towards a preoccupation with the renewal of the physical fabric of inner city areas . . .'[38]

By 1993 Professor Brian Robson of Manchester University, commissioned by the Department of the Environment, was forced to conclude the awful truth: that things had been getting, not better, but much, much worse. 'The biggest and most deprived urban areas have generally experienced a continuing deterioration,' he said. Indeed, 'the real value of government expenditure in a national sample of 123 city districts, including all the original 57 Urban Programme areas, fell by about *half* in real terms in the ten years between 1979 and 1989' (my italics).[39] The so-called 'black community' gets singled out for its relative lack of involvement in and benefit from urban policy in general – despite seemingly endless attempts to rectify the fact.[40] Such a criticism bespeaks far more a failure in understanding of what it means to be whole, a spiritual gap, than a failure of resolve or finance.

Despite the huge sums spent, things have been getting worse, and officialdom has known about it. The Bradford Report says of its data: 'None of this material is new; indeed, our disappointment is that it is of long standing' (Para. 1.8.2). '. . . widespread ignorance can be understood as an unfortunate stage in a difficult transitional process of groups from different traditions learning to live together. It has lasted for too long, and it must now be rapidly supplanted by knowledge' (Para. 2.2.2).

If the creation of the ICRC is a bid in the direction of increased understanding, it should be welcomed, and watched. It may be a tenative and controversial innovation in Britain's long history of Church/State partnership, but it could be an imaginative response to the urgent task of the hour: addressing the deep fissures that cut across British contemporary life which result in many places from an identity crisis that cannot be treated by cash, quangos or the mantra-like repetition of economic platitudes and anti-racist jargon. People are more than 'the economy'. You cannot ultimately bank on souls.

The issue for the Church in the multicultural millennium is not so much the 'Islamization' of a once-Christian culture as the emergence, with state collusion, of discrete territories where vastly different norms prevail, shut off and sometimes resentful, a breeding ground for ferment and a target for hostility. The discreteness of these territories exists not just by the 'accident' of settlement but by dint of prevailing legislative and intellectual norms. The Bradford Commission Report makes one fleeting but telling reference to politicized Muslim activists who, it is clear, are not 'responsible' for creating impenetrable Muslim colonies, but who are waiting in the wings to foment social unrest if matters are ignored much longer.[41] The report quotes one 'experienced Asian Councillor' as saying: 'These fringe religious groups have been agitating the youth for some time and played a significant role in the disturbance' (Para. 5.25.1). The report's writers feel it necessary to warn:

> It is not the radical nature of the extremists' beliefs . . . that is of concern to us . . . It is when the ideas and ideals are linked to the seizure of temporal power that freedom for all becomes endangered . . . It is one thing to say, as the adherents of many faiths would, that faith should guide societal, as well as individual, transactions. It is quite another to urge the destruction of secular society, the only possible basis for a multi-faith city . . . Ignorance is the fertile source of extremism, and there is a lot of ignorance around. (Paras 5.25.9, 10, 11)

13
An Islamic Vision for Britain?

If mainstream culture is bereft of vision, what of other 'cultures' within it? There is no such thing as 'an Islamic vision for Britain'. There are books and papers expressing religious aspirations whose passion is at odds with the *ad hoc* nature of Muslim settlement in the West. Never before in history have Muslims voluntarily migrated in large numbers into the lands of the unbeliever to seek its protection and prosperity. Islam classically divides the world into the House of Islam and the House of Unbelief – *Dar-ul-Kufr*, also meaning 'Abode of War' – and Muslims are enjoined to flee the defilement of the latter if for some reason they find themselves in it.[1]

Most Muslims did not come with a religious vision: they came for economic reasons, and the *maulvis* (scholars) and the *pirs* (holy men) followed later. Nonetheless, their stay is justified by some scholars in terms of *dawah* (missionary activity), rendering apt a wider debate about a vision for Britain to which this book is a contribution. This section therefore touches on this key factor behind Muslim self-consciousness in Britain – *dawah* – which distinguishes it from other ethnic or religious groups, such as Sikhs, Jews or Hindus, for example, for whom religion has more to do with birthright than with evangelism. Buddhism is an exception but is largely a white, middle-class phenomenon in Britain.

The Dutch scholar P. S. van Koningsveld has coined the expression '*Dar ul Dawah*' (the House of Mission) for this unprecedented scenario.[2] Muslim writers use the concept of *dawah* to give credibility to Muslim presence in the midst of so much unbelief. The

Guardian journalist Kalim Siddiqui, now deceased, wrote in *The Muslim Manifesto*:

> Performing *dawah* or inviting non-Muslims to accept Islam, is a basic duty of all Muslims. Muslims have come to live in the west in large numbers at a time when the western civilization is beginning to develop disorders of the mind, body and soul as a direct consequence of unmitigated secularism. In this situation the role of dawah is clear. However, the method of dawah is often and unnecessarily contentious among Muslims. There are those who take the passive route, and there are those who believe in working through revolutionary change, beginning with Muslim societies and countries. In Britain, in the short-term, the greatest impact is likely to be achieved through the example of moral and material excellence set by Muslim individuals and families living in a post-Christian, largely pagan, society. The collective effort of the Muslim community in Britain to lead a muttaqi [God-fearing, pious] life in a corrupt environment is bound to play a major role in dawah. Similarly, the taqwa [piety] of Muslim youth, the modesty of Muslim women, the stability of Muslim family life, the absence of drink-, drugs- and sex-related crimes and the overall discipline of Muslims living in the west will itself send powerful signals to non-muslims. But this will only happen if we succeed in arresting the 'integration' and 'assimilation' of Muslims themselves into the corrupt bogland of western culture and supposed 'civilization'. The emergence of a distinctive Muslim presence, individual and collective, is an essential first step towards effective dawah.[3]

Another Muslim scholar, Khurram Murad, described as 'one of the architects of current Islamic resurgence' worldwide, produced an 'action plan' for Britain that has been regarded as a significant indication of aspirations in some circles.[4] He was the second Director General of the Islamic Foundation in Leicester, held important posts in the world of international Islam, including that of Vice President of the ideological reform movement founded in 1941, the Jamaat-i-Islami in Pakistan. His death in Glenfield Hospital,

Leicester, in December 1996 was the cover story in the 7 February issue of *Q News*, self-styled as 'Britain's leading Muslim magazine', in which he received a nine-page 'appreciation' (three-quarters of it an article by the Christian American scholar Larry Poston).

His speeches are said to 'have inspired thousands of young men and women all over the world . . .' and, as an active resource-person in training programmes in the UK and America, played 'a key role in the character-building of the youth in the Islamic Movement.'[5] His most widely publicized work, *Islamic Movement in the West: Reflections on Some Issues*, is a useful summary of his ideas.

For him the Islamic Movement was 'an organised struggle to change the existing society into an Islamic Society based on the Quran and the Sunna and make Islam, which is a code for entire life [*sic*], supreme and dominant, especially in the sociopolitical spheres'. He states that 'the movement in the West should reaffirm and re-emphasise the concept of total change and supremacy of Islam in the Western society as its ultimate objective and allocate to it the highest priority'.

He was a pragmatic thinker: he recognized that capture of institutional bases of power is unlikely in the new diaspora. Thus, Muslims should both seek to influence those who do have power and to carry on the struggle at the local level. 'The ultimate objective of the Islamic movement shall not be realised unless the struggle is made by the Locals. For it is only they who have the power to change society into an Islamic society.' Participation in *dawah*, according to Murad but contrary to the opinion of some other scholars,[6] is obligatory in the Qur'ān. (Suras 3:187, 110; 5:159–60; 22:77–8.) Force should be an ultimate sanction, only in the establishment of justice, after Sura 57:25.

> We verily sent Our messengers with clear proofs, and revealed with them the Scripture and the Balance, that mankind may observe right measure; and He revealed iron, wherein is mighty power and (many) uses for mankind, and that Allah may know him who helpeth Him and His messengers, though unseen. Lo! Allah is strong, Almighty.[7]

'There can be no more categorical a statement regarding the central place that the Quran gives to establishing justice among people; in social structures, and between nations and to the mission of striving for this objective, even using force to dislodge powers that have become gods,' writes Murad.

The Islamic Foundation has been a significant spur to young Muslim identity-formation in Britain, with three particularly important offshoots with influence on university campuses: the student movement, Young Muslims UK; the Islamic Society of Britain; and a newspaper, *Trends*, edited by a female convert, Sarah Joseph, a graduate of the London School of Economics. Murad and his achievement reflect the ideological dynamic of the founder of the movement, the *Jamaat-i-Islami*, with which he was most identified: Seyyid Abu'l Ala Maududi, who was honoured at his death both by Pakistan and by Saudi Arabia.

Much has been written about Maududi's thought, but until 1996 there had been little if any detailed analysis in the context of its migration to and implications for Britain.[8] Derby University-based former convert Ahmed Andrews' discussion based on his survey of Muslim and British leadership attitudes to the Jamaat-i-Islami in Britain is an interesting exception. On the basis of research he carried out in 1987–8 at the Islamic Foundation in Leicester while he was a member of the UK Islamic Mission, he makes the contention that the organization is driving a wedge between ordinary non-politicized, 'working-class' Muslims – as he puts it – and mainstream society; '. . . to avoid the resistance Jamaat-i-Islami encounters from most sections of the Muslim community, it has decided to propagate its ideology within the host community by targeting religious and educational establishments in order to affect the host community's perception of Islam'.[9] Whatever the merits of Andrews' case, it has to be acknowledged that the Jamaat-influenced organizations are signalling the important issues for young Muslim intellectuals in Britain.

Maududi was a fundamentalist in Ron Geaves' useful definition of a word that has degenerated into both an offensive propaganda weapon against deeply held conviction as well as a description of political opportunism and even terrorism. It is essentially, Geaves concludes, 'a modern phenomenon which attacks the ideology of modernism'. It is characterized by idealism, zealotry and pragmatism. The peculiar nature of the Muslim profile in Britain can arguably be attributed to Maududi. An Indian-born journalist and self-taught scholar and activist, he is said by various authorities to be the most widely read Muslim writer in the world today[10] and the most important inspiration to the rising generation of Muslim thinkers in Britain.[11]

His significance lies not so much in the purgative virulence of his anti-Western writings as in the way he harnessed Western concepts to his ideals. He had his cake and ate it. He borrowed words like democracy, economy and legislature, which have a different or non-existent provenance in Islam. And he utilized technological developments like the mass media – despite their despised origins. He thus legitimized the Westernization of Islam, in the interests of Islamizing the West. He translates easily into the modern idiom, even if, in so doing, he has created scope for confusion over motive and meaning.

Maududi also believed that political power was essential for Muslim self-realization. Although consumed with a passion for God and his righteousness, only one of his 120 publications deals purely with theology. His radicalism led him to admire extreme political movements, even Western ones, especially Marxism and Fascism, and he sought to wipe away all but the first 15 years of Islamic history as being authentic. All else was venality, compromise and error. Extremism, ideological purity that uses religious symbols for political rather than spiritual ends – and a pragmatic blurring of conceptual boundaries – all make Maududi and those he influences today dangerous in the eyes of many Muslims, and disproportionately visible to the wider public in Britain.

14
Religious Rights and the Sharī'ah

Sharī'ah Law for Britain?

To be Muslim is to observe the Sharī'ah – the body of laws which together constitute the way to Paradise in the afterlife. The law is based actually and by derivation on what Allah revealed through Muhammad in the Qur'ān, and also, because that set him apart as a special (though not divine) human being, on reliable reports of what he said and did (collectively known as the *hadith*). Four schools of jurisprudence are tolerated within the Sharī'ah system, and geography largely determines which is observed.

The Sharī'ah is both a system of laws and a moral philosophy for the individual. It therefore governs what the West would divide into the two realms of public and private, and makes of them a whole. Islam, contrary to popular conception, is not a 'political religion', in the sense that the Qur'ān and the Sunnah (the normative, exemplary words and deeds of Muhammad not considered to be revelatory) do not lay down principles of any specific form of statehood or government. No concept of 'the state' has evolved because there is arguably no differentiated 'public' space, no 'civil society'. Islam is 'a religion that stresses above all the *collective* enforcement of *private morals*'.[1] Islam concerns itself minutely with the detail of domestic life, and the safeguarding of this is not a personal but a public duty.[2] And in that sense it has become highly political. The protection of the administration of the Sharī'ah requires temporal power and is thus the proper, and only, business of rulers as a means of aiding Muslims to reach heaven. Islam does not exist except in terms of the Sharī'ah, and the push for its implementation in some officially recognized form in Britain is inevitable.

The demand for the Sharī'ah to be incorporated into English law was first made during the 1970s by the Union of Muslim Organisations of UK and Eire (UMO). They sought official recognition of a separate system of Islamic family law which would automatically be applicable to all British Muslims. The UMO represented 150 different Muslim organizations at that time. They submitted the resolution to various government ministers with a view to its being enacted by Parliament. The move failed completely. It was, says Menski, 'a maximal response to a maximal demand'. A more gradual approach would be more likely to succeed.

A typically British accommodation has been taking place ever since in a vaguely permissive human rights atmosphere (Britain is, at the time of writing, a signatory to the European Convention on Human Rights, though its rulings are only admissible in the courts once tested in Strasbourg). The English legal system turns a blind eye to any ethnic law, so long as it does not actively violate English law. Minority religious 'rights' under religious freedom provisos have not been adequately tested in the Court of Human Rights, but this would face further debate once the Convention is incorporated fully into British law under new proposals. In theory, the right of religious belief and observance are officially guaranteed, but not such elements of religious praxis as conflict with existing provisos.

Werner Menski says: 'People purport to follow English law but in reality they are following what they understand *sharī'ah* to be. I have very clear evidence that people simply say and act accordingly, in terms of following *sharī'ah* first, placing that as superior to what our state legal system sets.' Furthermore, there are local legal variants. It matters Islamically whether you live in Bradford or Burnley.

Historical precedent (legal pluralism in family matters was given statutory force by the British Parliament during the Raj), and plural systems in parts of Asia and Africa today, lend weight to the likelihood of the adoption of some of the Sharī'ah, with the likelihood of a genuine 'clash of laws' in some points. Some detailed analysis has been done. Sebastian Poulter, Reader in Law at Southampton University, concludes that the role of women has changed so profoundly in modern cultures that to 'return to the Sharī'ah' would entail real challenges to both systems. Poulter looks at marriage and sees how Jews and Quakers are exempted from all regulations governing the solemnization of marriage under the Marriage Acts 1949–86. But he notes that whereas in the eighteenth century the privileges accorded to Jews and Quakers reflected religious *toleration*, in the new multicultural atmosphere of the twentieth century they have symbolized religious *discrimination*, and provide grist to that mill.

One clash that could theoretically arise if the Sharī'ah were to be merged with English law, is that Muslim marriages may occur without the bride and bridegroom actually being present. And arranged marriages do not require the assent of a 'minor' if the bride's guardian has approved it.[3] Poulter goes sympathetically through this and other aspects of family law: divorce, custody of children, and female circumcision (an Arab custom enshrined by *hadith* through the medieval practice of *ijma* or consensus of the learned men). Female circumcision was prohibited in the English statue books only in 1985. Poulter also covers education, financial provision on divorce and separation, inheritance (under Muslim law the share of a surviving wife as an heir is one eighth of the net estate unless there are children, in which case it is increased to one quarter).

Poulter finally shows which rules would be particularly unwelcome in view of the achievement of sexual equality – 'a matter of deep concern in modern Britain'.

> Examples of rules that are unlikely to find favour here for this reason are those permitting polygamy, forced marriages (as opposed to arranged marriages), marriages of girls before puberty and divorce through unilateral repudiation by the husband (*talaq*) as well as the ban on Muslim women marrying non-Muslim husbands.[4]

He speculates that the government's rejection in 1983 of the Sharī'ah was discriminatory, but convincing 'if it asserts that a basically uniform system has helped in the past to create a more cohesive society and . . . as part of the process of nation-building required to integrate the newer minorities into the general framework of English life and some of its most important values'. He concludes: 'to allow one religious denomination to separate itself off completely in this manner might be felt to be unacceptably divisive'.

The argument still has to be won among older influential Muslims. For the young, family law issues are evolving in what might be called the 'Islamization of change', which I look at in the next chapter. Rather than defend the old order, they are claiming that the new is Islamic.

Religious Rights

Despite racism, Muslim identity is sufficiently consolidated in Britain to act as a basis for negotiation for legal concessions. In 1995, Muslim activists, including the UK Action Committee on Islamic Affairs, *Muslim News* and *Q News* lobbied the Home Secretary for new religious concessions in existing discrimination legislation. The proposed offence, indicated by the words (in my italics) added to the existing clause on race, would have been:

> a) Public incitement to *discrimination*, violence or racial hatred in respect of the group of persons or a member of such a group defined by reference to colour, race, *religion*, or national or ethnic origin ... (Council for Racial Equality, Press Release, November 1995)

Other groups were lobbying other members of the European Union, such that it was raised as a 'Joint Action' by the European Interior Ministers meeting in Brussels in October 1995. Britain, whose veto is under pressure from majority voting, was alone out of the 15 member states in vetoing the move, which was otherwise conceded. The measure then went to Madrid for further discussion by the Heads of Government. The Council for Racial Equality (CRE) complained that there had been insufficient public debate about a measure which it reckoned went beyond existing terms of reference in dealing with minority affairs.

Michael Howard is believed to have changed his mind on the issue at the last moment after it was put to him that under such a provision Salman Rushdie could have been prosecuted for *The Satanic*

Verses. He later agreed in principle to bring in the requisite legislation once evidence had been mustered to demonstrate sufficient instances of religious discrimination. The CRE is undertaking a second nationwide data-gathering exercise, after the first failed to find sufficient data.

The CRE was uneasy about the move to extend race relations legislation to religion – and was criticized for being 'anti-Muslim' as a result.[5]

Papers leaked to *Q News* revealed that the Commission's lawyers regarded the 'joint action' as 'neither feasible nor desirable'. How do you define religion for the purposes of an Act? Does one include Druids or Moonies? There are practices sanctioned or forbidden by religions that society as a whole might find repugnant. The 1992 review of the 1976 Race Relations Act which, unlike the original, for the first time took religious discrimination seriously into account, spoke of 'ramifications going well beyond the area of good race relations'. Should religious demands, in a democracy, be based on the numbers who want them? Do 'group rights' supercede individual rights? Multiculturalism, religiously consolidated, makes this a likely option to the secular mind, unless a way is found to expand the rights debate to something more profound. 'Since there is no 'cross-cultural truth' or standard, there is no way to verify – or more importantly, to falsify – a group's claims,' say the multiculturalists.[6] Here is the real theological challenge.

15
Secularization and Assimilation

Multiculturalism may give minority groups the dignity and confidence to negotiate with the majority culture on their own terms. It may also lock individuals, and particularly women, into social blocs. What then is the scope for integration? This chapter examines some of the writing and research into the influence of secularism on Islam in the British diaspora to gauge what the future might hold.

A definition or two is in order. To *integrate* means to make one whole of many disparate parts – or more interestingly, 'to complete an imperfect thing by the addition of parts' (*OED*, 1976 edn.). Integrity is a moral attribute, a virtue, ascribed to a focused personality, and presumably integration is to be desired among the many persons that make up a society though its focus is an open question, and the subject of this book. Multiculturalism seems to deny the possibility of any focus. Australia's version of pluralism is described as settlement in 'a mosaic pattern', meaning lots of small bits living side by side, though the picture that is formed is not yet clear. To *assimilate* on the other hand is defined as 'to become like', or 'to take into oneself' (*Chambers Dictionary*). Both prospects alarmed Kalim Siddiqui, but assimilation is considered the greater evil among Muslim thinkers – and official pronouncements that seem to exhort it are counterproductive. In reality, a slow process of mutual accommodation appears to be both necessary and inevitable for both young Muslims and mainstream society as we shall see, but its painfulness is made worse by the difficult nature of the issues for policy-makers without a religious vocabulary.

Kalim Siddiqui, recently deceased founder of the Khomeini-inspired Muslim Parliament (*Majlis al-Shura-al-Islami fi Britanniya*), made it a premise of that organization's *Manifesto* that 'the option of "integration" and/or "assimilation" that is on offer as official policy in Britain must be firmly resisted and rejected.'[1] The Parliament as it was under Siddiqui is not taken seriously by some Muslims such as Zaki Badawi, al-Azhar-educated[2] chairman of the Imams and Mosques Council UK and the UK Muslim Law Council, who dismissed it as a 'pantomime'.[3] Nonetheless, some of its high-profile pronouncements project a sense of difference in a manner that gives succour to those who wish to find a reason to fear Muslims in Britain; and its name guarantees it 'irritant value' for the British media. Tariq Modood notes that 'for better or for ill [it] colours majority–minority relations in Britain'.[4] The Muslim Parliament bases its distinctiveness firmly on religion. Massoud Shadjareh, chair of the 'Parliaments' Human Rights Committee says: 'Our identity is first and foremost religious.'[5]

Syed Ali Ashraf, General Editor of *Crisis in Muslim Education*, a compilation of papers read at the First World Conference on Muslim Education, organized by King Abdulaziz University in Mecca in 1977, shows the deep ramifications of a religious identity for the true Muslim in his introductory remark that, 'It can be seen that religious groups are no longer dominating the social scene in the West and hence all branches of knowledge have no central, integrating force.' With a note of desperation he adds: '. . . if the intellectuals of the Muslim world do not stem the tide now by instilling Islamic concepts in all branches of knowledge and changing the methodology from unbridled questioning, to the exploration of the significance of everything for the sake of understanding Human Life and External Nature, the time is not far away when the tide will sweep away even the bedrock on which the structure of Muslim society is based'.[6] He talks of Western 'brainwashing', rootlessness and later, in relation to a dual allegiance in education to Western and Islamic values, of bloodshed and bitterness. He hits an almost Messianic note when he describes the 'extreme value to the whole Western world of a radical new programme for the Islamisation of education which will build intellectual inquiry on the firm basis of a faith in divine revelation'. Much

Muslim writing conveys this sense of angst about the desacralization of the world. It usually expresses itself as a contempt for Western 'values', which are seen as corrupting, threatening and destructive of the revealed divine truth that binds people together.

In 1976, in response to the first multi-faith syllabus in Britain published by the City of Birmingham, the Union of Muslim Organisations published their own widely quoted syllabus. It stated: 'Any child who has gone through the lessons prepared along the guidelines given above is expected to have built within himself or herself the positive power to resist the disintegrating and degenerating forces of modern civilization and gain certainty and peace of mind . . .' It goes on to assert the aspiration that each child shall 'carry on a campaign for true Jihad (struggle in the path of Allah the Almighty)'. Nonetheless, commentators observe that the godless 'Western system' of thought which they so resent has produced science and technology and with those, wealth. 'It is clearly understood that there can be no question in the present age of rejecting modern science and technology. One cannot ask the community to go back to the days of isolation, nor will such a policy work if Muslims have to live in organised societies and free themselves from the oppressive burden of poverty and material backwardness. They must acquire the secrets which have led elsewhere to miraculous transformations.'[7]

Weber believed those secrets to have been largely religiously derived. He particularly identified Protestantism's sense of duty or 'calling': hard work, the early Calvinists believed, did not save you, but was indicative that your salvation had been effected. Weber also singled out the disciplines of open accounting, saving and, perhaps the most important of all, the severing of the feudal and patriarchal stranglehold on society through free association of all orders of men and eventually women in urban churches. Gellner believes these characteristics exist in Islam and could lend themselves to an Islamic 'economic miracle'.

Another scholar who has studied the Islamic religious reaction in Britain to secularism is Stephen Barton, whose study of the sermons of a Bradford *imam* shows a fascinating attempt at Islamic entrenchment in the face of a voluntary exile. He records the *imam*'s expressed role as to protect the community from secularism. 'In teaching

Islam, the imam aims to purge the Bengali Muslims of syncretism, to instil in them the concept of Islam as a complete code of life, and to prevent them from becoming secularized.'[8] This *imam* sees the Qur'ān school and the institution of *purdah* as the main defences against secularism. But Barton notes that the *imam*'s influence and wishes may be limited by the inability of his listeners to understand him since his addresses are given in high Bengali, rather than their Sylheti dialect – a common practice.

As far as Low Islam is concerned, the separation of belief from the practices that have mediated it is recognized to be the problem. The gap between Allah and worshipper, usually filled by *pirs* or local saints, remains unfilled except where such people have migrated with their communities. Even so, the twin pressures of reformist Islam in seeking to purge the faith of accretions, and secularism, which has rendered superstition redundant since the forces of nature no longer need to be manipulated, have led commentators like Kenneth Cragg to conclude that the crisis facing Muslim communities in the modern world is one of knowing not what to believe, but how to believe. 'If the former traditions of a community are no longer available or powerful, they must be modified or replaced if religious faith is to survive.'[9] The strict maintenance of *purdah* which the *imam* recommends could promote what he wants to avoid: widening the generation gap between women and their more adventurous daughters, leading to the disintegration of family and community through 'depressive isolation'.

The defensiveness represented by the Qur'ān school – of which there are several thousand in Britain, many funded by local authorities, and which use only Arabic, incomprehensible to most children – could actually cause secularization. By seeking to avoid a society it sees as promoting fragmentation, it reinforces itself as a fragment: 'the pressures of secular society may render the Qur'an school merely a token of cultural identity', writes Barton. This is echoed by Husain and Ashraf when describing the Al-Azhar in Cairo, the Muslim world's most prestigious academic institute: 'Its syllabuses have not undergone any change for centuries with the result that when under the impact of its contact with the West, Egypt woke up, it discovered that what Al-Azhar offered was very largely irrelevant to its contemporary needs.'[10] It played however 'an extremely important role in the maintenance of Islam . . .' Such institutions play a vital symbolic role in the survival of Islam. W. A. Shadid and P. S. van Koningsveld also note: 'Despite the existing differences in the perception of Islam, their Islamic background will increasingly become a common-identity symbol to these migrants, differentiating them from the hostile society surrounding them. In other words, Islam will come to the foreground, not as an entity of religious rituals and behavioural rules, but as a *symbol* of a separate identity.'[11]

Alison Shaw's four-year doctoral study of 130 east-Oxford households, concluded in 1988, identifies a surprising loyalty by second-generation Pakistanis to the demands of family and *biradari* (clan). Resistance to arranged marriages, and prejudice among parents against girls studying, appear on the face of it to be no more or less than are normal for the culture, whether in Pakistan or Britain. As has been noted earlier, the free movement of young people to and from Pakistan acts as a conservative force on the second generation, since they are exposed to peer as well as parental pressure. But there are subtle changes: Shaw notes a new phenomenon that addresses the question of assimilation. She observes girls pursuing careers *and* earning the blessing of their parents: 'The way in which girls argue that they remain true to their culture owes much to their western upbringing. They justify their careers by reference to religious ideology, arguing that their critics' understanding of Islam is outdated . . . inappropriate in Pakistan too . . .' This might be termed the 'Islamization of change'. These girls are 'pioneers of a new pattern', neither simply traditional nor Western. She also notes young men Islamizing their resistance to tradition. She quotes 'Hasan':

> I have nothing personally against the girl they had chosen for me – I'm sure she is very nice – but I didn't want to marry a girl who has come straight from Pakistan, who doesn't know English, and knows nothing of my life here. My parents are living in the 1960s. They arrange marriages with relatives not according to our religion but to keep property in the family; they regard women as property. In our religion, it is wrong to force someone to marry. Both the girl and the boy should

> be asked if they consent. But very often our people don't even ask, they just go ahead because the marriage is in their interests, expecting everybody to agree so that no one loses face. That's all they think about, their face, not whether what they're doing is right or wrong in the religion. Our Muslim nikah (marriage ceremony) is a contract between a man and a woman who have to consent to the marriage in front of witnesses, that's all. You don't have to marry your cousin, that's just tradition. And it's the couple who have to give their consent, not the parents.[12]

Hasan rejected his father's choice of bride, to marry Shamim. It split the family.

A major series of studies into Pakistani Muslims in Britain by French scholar Danièle Joly, published in 1995, before the Bradford riots, also found that change in identity was happening although it remained rooted in religion. One survey, based on interviews with 22 young Kashmiris in Birmingham over four years, concluded: 'All the young people stated when asked about their identity, "I am a Muslim." ' He quotes one youth saying: 'What makes me think I am a Pakistani?: – the religious way of thinking.'

Joly comments: 'Living and being brought up in a non-Muslim society has not overturned the beliefs and practices of young Pakistanis. They are Muslims and want to remain as such, although sometimes seeking a better and more critical understanding of the religion as it is taught to them.'[13] Birmingham Muslims were not alienated from British society, he concluded, finding in it an inspiration for change. But he also noted pressure building up from a combination of unemployment, discrimination, and conservatism demonstrated over Salman Rushdie's *Satanic Verses* which 'for the first time revealed the participation of a substantial number of young Muslims in public protest'. The Bradford riots served to emphasize the point.

Shadid and van Koningsveld believe that the relation between Church and State is critical to the full integration of Muslims and Hindus – which they term 'emancipation'. 'It is clear that norms and values of a Christian background are in a privileged position, whereas those derived from Islam have to fight themselves in.'[14]

Shadid and Lewis both note, however, that divisions within the Muslim communities themselves militate against their efforts towards political establishment which strikes at the very heart of Islamic faith and leads, presumably, to considerable psychological dislocation. Lewis, for example, noted in 1994 that although 11 of the 51 members in the ruling Labour group on Bradford City Council are Muslim (more than 20 per cent), the city still has not returned a Muslim MP.[15] Shaw also notes that differences over religious doctrine are often of more importance to so-called community leaders than, for example, the council's housing policy.[16]

Shadid and Koningsveld note the difficulties Muslims face in presenting an identifiable political identity: 'The ethnical [*sic*] and religious diversity of these organisations, as well as their being focussed on their countries of origin, not only weaken their position in relation to their host Governments but also impede these particular Governments in applying one and the same policy with regard to Islam.' Shaw finds other difficulties: that those considered by mainstream powerbrokers to be representatives are often not so regarded by the communities, or even by the *biradaris* they purport to represent. The cultural notion of 'patronage', vulnerable to corruption and dependent more on the show of power than its reality, has transferred from the countries of origin. Muslim representation will continue to be problematic. The recent foundation of the Muslim Council of Britain, under the leadership of Cambridge academic and broadcaster Akhbar Ahmed, which received very mixed reviews from British Muslims themselves, is unlikely to resolve the situation.

Iqbal Sacranie, Joint Convenor the UK Action Committee on Islamic Affairs and a member of the Home Secretary's Advisory Council on Race Relations, on Radio 4's *Sunday Programme*, welcomed the move as a way to 'deal directly with the government' on 'religious discrimination'. The Muslim Parliament on the other hand dismissed it as a 'frantic' attempt by a post-colonial government to 'control Islam and Muslims'.[17]

The answer, believes Tariq Modood, lies in the state itself changing in order to accommodate Muslims *qua* Muslims – what he calls 'centripetal institutions' – so that Muslims are not simply regarded as divisive. The state, he argues, must allow religions to flourish, by the introduction of legislation against religious discrimination (as yet undefined), and by extending the range of religious schools and education within the state system. He believes the state must be shaped around religious as well as other communities.[18] He dismisses arguments in favour of religious disestablishment put forward by commentators like Shadid and Koningsveld while acknowledging its logic: that if faith is the primary identity of any community, then that minority cannot fully identify with and participate in a polity that privileges a 'rival faith'. However, says Modood, the alternative – radical secularism – privileges, not a religion, but a philosophy of religion that is at odds with the increasingly vocalized demands of faith.[19]

If, as Sanneh shows, 'freedom is ultimately an act of faith', it is the Church's vital role to continue to remind the state of that fact, particularly in a time of unsettled, even potentially tumultuous social change. The preserving, leavening influence of the Church uniquely established at the heart of public life, but in no position to dominate or coerce it, may be the only way of rescuing the very notion of freedom of conscience – whether you look at it from a secular or a Christian standpoint.

Religious plurality is a fact. How far that extends in practice – and becomes 'plural-ism' – is still an open question and one that has to be debated in light of the ethos and tradition which it is the Church's missionary task to maintain and proclaim.

If multiculturalism means the practical espousal of the equality of all cultures and therefore equality of the religions that have shaped and informed them, then all beliefs and practices deserve not just equal respect but equal space. Christians must decide for themselves whether this is the kind of society they can endorse. And society as a whole must decide whether the multiculturalism it seeks to celebrate is honestly so, and is not in fact just a guise for covert assimilationism into 'our way of life'. The Church with its patient, permissive constraints stands as a sign of the diversity of the Father's good creation and of the Oneness into which we will all grow up.

It could well be argued that pluralism, limited by existing laws in terms of unacceptable elements of social and religious praxis (religious discrimination in employment and housing, Islamophobia, female abduction, polygamy, clitoridectomy) and guaranteed by a state church acting as a broker[20] for religion within the secular polity, is not only a more likely way forward than total assimilation, but the only realistic one.

16

Islamophobia and the Church

Islamophobia

November 1997 saw the publication of a major report by the Runnymede Trust's Commission *British Muslims and Islamophobia.* It recommended changes in the law to 'confront and reduce' 'dread or hatred of Islam and of Muslims'. It marked a further stage in the de-privatization of religion.

There are seven features of 'Islamophobia' – a word coined, it is believed, in the Nineties by the Policy Studies Institute, along the lines of xenophobia and homophobia, making a pathological and politicized category out of a problematic social phenomenon – shifting the responsibility for fear from the equivocal cause of it to the unequivocal sufferer from it. These features are:

- Muslim cultures are seen as monolithic and unchanging;
- claims that Muslim cultures are wholly different from other cultures;
- Islam perceived as implacably threatening;
- claims that Islam's adherents use their faith mainly for political or military advantage;
- Muslim criticisms of Western cultures and societies rejected out of hand;
- fear of Islam mixed with racist hostility to immigration;
- Islamophobia assumed to be natural and unproblematic.

That it is Muslim groups rather than Hindu, Sikh or Rastafarian who have succeeded in making such a significant political issue of their cultural and religious distinctiveness is testimony both to that distinctiveness and to the scale of the problem.

Religion is a significant political issue for mainland Britain again, affecting the social order demographically, legally, geographically ('the Islamization of space', i.e. mosques and community centres) and in public service provision. 'Identity is wrapped up with religious belonging',[1] and if that is the case, the ghost in Weber's machine – his 'dead religious beliefs'[2] – is undead, and stalking the public arena both because of increased migration and because of the wider human identity crisis that secularization has caused. Christians cannot ignore their responsibility to re-enter that arena with a clear voice. If legal decisions are being made on the basis of the numbers demanding them, then any vision of the future could be increasingly fragmented, if not fraught. True faith does not distinguish itself by its populism. God is sovereign, and to legislate on any basis other than his revealed will denies the life-giving prophetic element in religion that rises above human limitation and political expediency. True Muslims, like true Christians, are ultimately made, not born – and the banal statistical comparisons that emerge from time to time often degrade the discussion. Numbers, however, are pivotal in a democracy, making informed debate urgent.

If religions wish a hearing in public life, they must earn it, as John Biffen observed in Parliament, during the furore which greeted the *Faith in the City* report in 1985, when it was dubbed Marxist and rejected as exceeding its remit. In response to Brian Mawhinney's complaint that 'the cabinet of Canterbury' was no place from which to seek political guidance, Biffen gracefully replied:

> the Church throughout the ages has sought to interest itself in social affairs, but if it does so, it has to accept that it will be judged in its contribution to the arguments by the quality it conveys to that argument.[3]

The same must be said for all 'faiths'. Without a better, and better-articulated, vision for society as a whole, which is more than simply a shared geography, the danger of a depersonalizing and even violent fragmentation happening by default, which some fear is the legacy of multiculturalism, is all too obvious.

To return to the Bradford Commission Report, in an unconsciously ironic echo of Norman Tebbit's much-ridiculed remark about cricket being the test of allegiance:

> The separate development of team sports leagues for Asians, particularly cricket, of which we have heard, is a symptom of divisions in the city which raises in an acute form the question, 'Do young Bradfordians of different ethnic backgrounds want to be entirely separate in their leisure activities, or not?' If they do, then there is little hope of harmonious relationships across what will be increasingly polarised groupings, as those young people become the mature citizens of the not-too-distant future. If they do not, what are those with the power to encourage joint participation doing about it? (Para. 5.29.2)

In Newcastle, signs are that such people are backing away. Nigel Todd, Labour Chairman of Newcastle City Council's Racial Equality Working Group and a professed atheist, says that councillors are being denounced whenever they resist Islamic exclusivism. 'If they don't get their way, they say you are racist. These are politically inspired accusations that are about achieving another agenda. The aggro is ruining people's lives. Why should we bother any more?'[4] Whether this perception is right or not barely matters: the liberal conscience is demonstrably weary. Race issues have been demoted from a big-spend committee in one city to a sub-committee of a sub-committee without a budget.

Race legislation, as Muslims are aware, has missed the point – and, in Bradford, has demonstrably failed.[5] The government's response to ethnic minority presence has been mostly reactionary grandiloquence. Muslim activism, regardless of its own distinctive religious centre of gravity, is using any of the weapons of the broader politics of group pride and ethnic assertiveness that come to hand in its bid to find a true home in Britain.[6] Britain's 'nightmare of pluralism' to use Ballard's ironic expression, is not going to fade away. The political fallout of the existence of different cultural, ethnic and racial groups, negotiating their collective identities in the face of the failure during two world wars of European cultural supremacy, cannot be wished away. 'Paki' cannot 'go home' because home is here. Britain is Pakistan, is India, is Nigeria – is us. And unless that is actively recognized by those with a vision of humanity that rises above the accidents of birth and the circumstances of history, unrest will intensify.

The debate will have to broaden. The situation is not a straight choice between assimilation (becoming 'like them') and multiculturalism (remaining as 'we' are) because neither is as straightforward as it seems – or, indeed, real. The old dualistic patterns of discourse are being forced to give way to a more nuanced awareness, and better pathways are required for those seeking to guide the nation in light of it. Multidisciplinary theologians with wide experience of mission and public service and who have earned the trust of the minorities among whom they live, people like David Randolph-Horn at the ICRC, Bishop Michael Nazir-Ali, who advises Prince Charles, and sociologist Philip Lewis in Bradford, will become increasingly needed as leaders cast around for answers. The Good News was given for times like these.

Amid all the criticism heaped upon institutions and service providers by Mohammed Taj in the wake of Bradford's riots, two paragraphs leap off the Report's page, pointing to both the need and the validity of a more vigorous and widespread espousal of a vision for Britain that is fired by all that the gospel is and stands for:

> It may be thought that the Christian Churches would have a limited role to play in a multi-ethnic area such as Manningham. On the contrary they have been committed and active in promoting good inter communal relationships and in speaking out on behalf of the poor and disadvantaged.
>
> The Anglican churches have shown particular vigour in this field and have maintained a considerable presence in the area, at a significant cost, with valuable effect. They deserve recognition from the wider community for their genuine goodwill and the positive effect of their efforts. (p. 14)

The Church, steeped in prayer, responding in service and fully imbued with the doctrine of loving self-emptying, has shown itself, even in the eyes of non-Christians, to be a uniquely significant bridge-builder to a future less frightening than that imagined by Ballard.

> Europe's Muslims have already begun to resist denigration and exclusion far more actively than did their predecessors [the Jews]. Though Europe's Muslim population is currently roughly similar in scale to that of pre-holocaust Jewry, their global presence is very much larger. If conflict should erupt across that disjunction . . . casualties would not be restricted only to one side . . . if Europeans choose to maintain their long-standing condition of denial, it is at their own peril.[7]

Muslims must be persistently enabled to take a full part in an intellectually rigorous public life in Britain. Their religious sensibility, and the cultural challenges that result, while often exposing them to criticism and hostility in wider society, could also act as a catalyst towards a more honest and searching social discourse about what is true. But the parochialism of much public comment about faith and justice must not be allowed to obscure the reality of gross inequities faced by religious dissidents in modern Muslim polities. Neither must it be allowed to obscure the grandeur and unpredictability of God's vision.

'Religion' may be a principle source of identity or community, but only the Man in whom we are all built up – Christ Jesus – can point us to the true source of identity. He sanctions by his grace what is valid in our diversity while commanding our allegiance to one another as creatures. It was the outcast Samaritans Christ chose to epitomize divine love. Virtue is non-denominational.

> Then the angel showed me the river of the water of life, as clear as crystal, flowing from the throne of God and of the Lamb down the middle of the great street of the city. On each side of the river stood the tree of life, bearing twelve crops of fruit, yielding its fruit every month. And the leaves of the tree are for the healing of the nations.

Part Four

A Light to the Nations: Theology in Politics

Lesslie Newbigin

17
The Demoralizing of Politics

The argument of the preceding chapters forces me to ask again the question about the possibility of a Christian society. In my experience the immediate reaction among Christians to this question is a negative one. Do you want to go back to the Middle Ages? Do you want to undo the great achievements of the Enlightenment and of the centuries which have followed? And, of course, the answer is 'No'. We cannot go back to the past even if we wished to, and we ought not to wish to do so. But this knee-jerk reaction has to be challenged. If we cannot go back, it is also certain that we cannot stand still. The present trends in the liberal democratic societies of the West are carrying us in a direction in which most decent human beings do not want to go. It is true that some proposals for a Christian society have failed to recognize that some of the achievements of the Enlightenment are positive gains which we can never surrender, above all the acknowledgement of the right to freedom of conscience in matters of religious belief. Perhaps, as Ian Markham argues, the Christendom Group led by V. A. Demant and others, in which T. S. Eliot was also involved, was guilty of this error.[1] We have to recognize that the Christian Church faces a new and unprecedented situation. A brief glance at history will serve in a preliminary way to make the point.

The Church of the first three centuries lived as a rejected minority within a pagan society. They held none of the levers of power. They were not in a position from which they could dream of a Christianized Roman Empire. But this did not mean that the Church confined itself to what is now called 'the private sector'. There was, as is well known, a great variety of religious cults offering salvation through various forms of religious practice, and their freedom was safeguarded. The Church did not avail itself of the protection provided for these private cults (*cultus privatus*). On the contrary, it openly challenged the public cult centred in the veneration of the Emperor as divine (*cultus publicus*). It refused to use the word 'Lord' (*kurios*) for the Emperor, on the ground that Jesus is the only one to whom this title may properly be applied. If it did not envisage a Christian society, it also refused to accept a pagan ideology for the public sector.

The Roman Empire shared with most ancient empires of which we have knowledge the character of what Arendt van Leeuwen called the 'ontocratic state'.[2] This term is meant to indicate the idea that the power exercised by the ruler of a great empire is not mere human power but embodies and represents the power of ultimate reality – however that may be conceived. This, one might say, is the most basic and primitive way of answering the question: How is political power to be legitimated? How does a ruler of an empire differ from a bandit whose only right to exercise power is his possession of exceptional power and ruthlessness? How otherwise can citizens be persuaded that they not only must, but ought to, submit to the rule of kings and emperors?

When in the fourth century AD the Emperor Constantine turned to the Christian Church as the only body capable of renewing the disintegrating pagan society, the Church inherited a political order which it had not created. It was still the same kind of society, with Christianity as the new *cultus publicus*. The former veneration of the Emperor had been the glue which was intended to keep this vast sprawling collection of tribes and peoples in some kind of unity. The new glue was now to be the Christian religion. It would be an obvious anachronism to suggest that, in this situation, the Church could have developed the concept of a liberal society in which religious belief would be a matter of purely personal concern.

Certainly the new situation was not a mere modification of the old ontocratic order. Society was to be one body with two distinct forms of rule. Church and society were one in respect of their constituent membership, but had distinct structures of authority. Although it would take many centuries and many bitter conflicts to develop the full implications of the teaching of Jesus and the apostles on the relations between these two ministries, both derived their authority from God. Disputes among churchmen about doctrine could not be settled by the Emperor, but it was his business to get them settled for the sake of the unity of society. The territorial principle was not in question; religion was part of the order of society.

The different political circumstances of the eastern and western parts of the empire led to different patterns of relationship between church and state. In Byzantium, the seat of both emperor and patriarch, the power of the former was relatively great. In the west, where Rome retained its almost magical aura of authority, there was no resident emperor and the authority of the Pope was relatively greater. The action of the Pope in creating a rival emperor in the west by crowning Charlemagne in AD 800 led (along with doctrinal causes) to the great schism of 1054 and the almost total separation of the two halves of Christendom. In both halves the territorial principle still prevailed and was not seriously threatened except in the disputed area of the Balkans. The bitterness of the resulting conflicts is (as we know from tragic events today) one of the most terrible legacies of Christian division.

The second great schism within the western half of Christendom occurred five centuries later. In respect of territoriality the division was not neat and clear as it was (apart from the Balkans) in the earlier schism. Europe was torn between two interpretations of the gospel and, although there was a rough line of division between northern and southern Europe, believers on both sides of the religious divide were living side-by-side in most parts of the continent. With the very important exception of the Anabaptists, those on both sides adhered without question to the territorial principle. The result was a patchwork of states, Lutheran, Roman Catholic, Reformed or Anglican, within each of which the governing authorities sought to enforce religious uniformity as encapsulated in the slogan *Cuius regio eius religio*.

This second great schism was to have consequences much more far-reaching than those which followed the schism of 1054. For most of the seventeenth century the soil of Europe was being soaked with the blood of Christians fighting each other with ferocious zeal on behalf of their rival interpretations of divine revelation. The result had been no victory for either side, but the division of the one household of western Christendom into two parties locked in apparently irreconcilable hatred and hostility, with the possibility of renewed war just under the surface. Much of the best intellectual leadership of Europe was sickened by this experience. At the same time, as the result of a number of factors, a new way of understanding the world in which we live was developing. It was a way of knowing which would increasingly come to appropriate for itself the Latin word of which 'knowledge' is an English form: the word 'science'. It was a way of knowing which did not depend on divine revelation but exclusively on the human powers of empirical observation and rational argument. Its most brilliant product was given to Europe just at the time when the long and bloody wars of religion were reaching their barren conclusion. Isaac Newton's *Principia Mathematica* offered a brilliantly clear and comprehensive picture of how things are, a picture which seemed to be capable in principle of explaining both the mysterious movements of the heavenly bodies and such homely events as the falling of an apple. It was the product of human observation and reason, and it could be understood by the exercise of the same human powers.

Here was a way by which Europe could escape from the cruel tyranny of religion and, in the century following Newton, it was adopted with growing enthusiasm. In the century which described itself as the Age of Reason, Europe embarked on a new path which would lead to the abandonment of the territorial principle in religion, which would recognize as public truth those things which can be established by the disciplined use of observation and reason, and which would leave questions of religious belief to the conscience of each person. From the point of view of this discussion, and leaving aside the best changes in the conditions of human life which have been brought about (in some parts of the world) by the application of science to human affairs, this shift had two immensely important results. First, it laid the grounds for a doctrine and practice of religious freedom. The right of every human being, irrespective of the place of birth or residence, to follow the dictates of conscience in matters of religious belief, at least in terms of religious observance, was affirmed. This remains one of the most remarkable and radical achievements of the Age of Reason. It was something radically new. It was not accepted by the Roman Catholic Church until the twentieth century. In much of Eastern Orthodoxy it has gained only a precarious hold, since ethnicity is still an immensely powerful element in the churches of Russia, Greece, Serbia and others. It is still rejected by Islam and is under attack by resurgent fundamentalist elements among Hindus. It is an achievement on which there can be no turning back.

The second crucially important effect of the revolution of the eighteenth century, a corollary of the first, is that religion is recognized to be a matter of personal commitment. One does not become a Christian by birth or residence alone. There has to be a personal response of faith and commitment at the deepest personal level. This kind of deep personal commitment is no longer to be a matter for those specially called to it, for monks and clergy. For everyone without exception there is the call to personal conversion and commitment.

These two, the rejection of the territorial principle and the call to personal holiness, are indeed the two sides of one coin. One may observe some of the implications by looking at the history of the European missionary enterprise. The early Roman Catholic missions in the New World were shaped by the territorial principle. They were, in a sense, a continuation of the struggle to expel the Muslim conquerors from Spain. The earliest Lutheran missions of the eighteenth century were likewise based on the territorial principle. They went to places under the rule of the Lutheran powers, primarily Denmark. By contrast, the great wave of Protestant missionaries, of whom William Carey is often seen as a paradigm, were typically men and women of the Enlightenment. They looked for individual conversion, not for the conversion of whole territories through the conversion of their rulers. Indeed, Protestant missionaries were initially forbidden by the Raj from entering India at all. Carey had to sail under the Danish flag and settle in the Danish territory of Serampore. And, of course, they claimed freedom for converts to practise a religion different from the one which ruled the territory where they worked.

The liberal doctrine of the state developed slowly from the end of the eighteenth century and, against the resistance of the older conception, through the nineteenth century. Its most powerful manifestation was in the creation of the new and unprecedented society of the United States of America. Here the territorial principle was decisively rejected. There was to be free exercise of religion as a matter of personal choice and subject to no kind of pressure from the state. But this doctrine of personal religious freedom was undergirded by a theological statement which represents the survival of the older Christian tradition. The great statement of the Declaration of Independence ascribes to the Creator the gift of the right of all people to life, liberty and the pursuit of happiness. But here is the point at which the liberal doctrine faces a problem.

During the nineteenth and twentieth centuries, this belief in a personal Creator came under mounting attack. As a matter of private belief it continued to hold the allegiance of many, perhaps most, of the inhabitants of the 'modern' world. But as something which could be appealed to in the course of debate about public policy it faded into silence. 'Human rights' came to be regarded as something inherent in human nature itself, without reference to their source in a divine Giver.

This means, as Professor Sanneh has so clearly argued, that the liberal doctrine of the state runs into a self-contradiction. As long as the claim for the rights of every human person is grounded in the gift of the divine Creator, they have a firm basis in reality. But if belief in the existence of God ceases to be part of public truth, if nothing exists except the totality of what is accessible to observation and reason, there would seem to be no grounds for affirming the rights of an individual against the collective, or of a minority against the majority. In the end, the collective must prevail over the individual units. Without any basis in a supernatural reality, the liberal state slides inevitably towards the rule of the collective, mobilized, as it can so easily be, by some ideology or some charismatic leader. But if the rights of the individual are to be grounded in the act of a divine Creator, it follows that the gift of these rights cannot be totally severed from an understanding of the end for which the gift was given. One cannot take divine action on an *à la carte* basis. If human rights are the gift of a personal Creator, they cannot be exercised forever without reference to the ends for which they were given. The concept of rights is a juridical one and is void of meaning except where there is a framework of mutual responsibilities mutually acknowledged. Without this the claim to human rights has as much validity as the writing of a cheque on a non-existent bank account.

For the same reason it is becoming increasingly clear that the attempt to establish liberal forms of the state in cultures which have quite different roots is proving to be very problematical. The liberal state is a product of the Judaeo-Christian tradition. When that tradition atrophies, the liberal state is threatened. When it is introduced into societies shaped by other traditions, the graft tends to be rejected – even when grants from the IMF and the World Bank are conditional upon its acceptance!

I think, therefore, that it is reasonable to say that the success of the liberal concept of the state in Europe and its outposts has been due to the continuing strength of the Christian tradition and that, as this tradition continues to weaken, we must expect the problems of liberalism to grow. We must, as Christians, acknowledge without reservation the fruits of the Enlightenment and above all its establishment of the principle of religious freedom. We have to confess that the Church had failed to recognize that the territorial principle was ultimately incompatible with the gospel, and it needed the bloody tragedy of the religious wars to awaken Europe to this fact. But this necessary gratitude and necessary penitence must not incapacitate us for seeing the roots of the present *malaise* of the 'modern' liberal state. There is an inconsistency at its root. A claim for the rights of the individual person grounded in the act of the divine Creator cannot be severed from the acknowledgement that this right is bound up with responsibility to the same Creator. The Enlightenment, while acknowledging the right of religious freedom for the individual, banished divine revelation from the arena of public truth. Here is the fundamental inner contradiction. This needs to be spelled out in respect of three matters.

1. From the Enlightenment until this day it is assumed by most people in the Western liberal societies that questions about the nature of God and his purpose for human life are undecidable and can only be matters of private opinion. Attempts to

affirm any view on these matters as public truth which everyone ought to believe are unacceptable. The tolerance afforded to all religious beliefs is therefore properly described rather as indifference than as tolerance – and Jenny Taylor has illustrated some of the fruits of that. Tolerance is the willingness to give space and freedom to beliefs which one considers to be false. The ultimate theological grounds for this tolerance have to be spelled out in a later part of this argument. This will bring us to the very heart of what is involved in the idea of a Christian society. But an agnostic indifference undercuts its own foundation. If the truth about the meaning and purpose of human life is something in principle unknowable, then there are no grounds for defending the liberal doctrine against any other doctrine of human nature and destiny. The helplessness of liberal societies in the face of militant religious fundamentalism amply illustrates this point. If the truth about these ultimate matters is unknowable, then there are no arguments except those of the gun and the bomb.

2. The belief that the nature and purpose of human life are in principle unknowable is the product of the rejection of divine revelation as a source of public truth in favour of empirical observation and rational argument on the basis of these observations. The elevation of these methods as the sole avenues to reliable public truth has the necessary consequence of excluding purpose as a category of explanation. A purpose, until it is fully realized, is known only to the one whose purpose it is. When the project has been completed, it is open to observation and rational argument. Until that time it can only be known if the one whose purpose it is makes it known. It is entirely possible to hold that there is no purpose; that this entire cosmos and human lives within it exist for no purpose at all (though the practical implications of taking this seriously boggle the mind). However, if there is any purpose in things other than the many contradictory purposes which millions of humans seek to pursue, then this purpose could only be known if the One whose purpose it is reveals it. There is no other possibility.

3. If the purpose for which things exist is unknowable, it follows that the words 'good' and 'bad' cease to have any ascertainable meaning. A thing may be good for one purpose but bad for another. If there is no publicly accepted belief about what human life is for, about its purpose, there is no way in which human conduct can be described as good or bad. Conduct becomes a matter of purely personal choice based on personally preferred 'values'. There are no barriers to halt the gradual slide into moral anarchy which liberal societies are witnessing at the present time.

18

Activating the Christian Vision

I have said that the continued health of liberal societies has been dependent on the continued strength of the Judaeo-Christian tradition to which numbers (though decreasing) adhere as a matter of personal choice. But because this adherence has been a matter for the individual and the intimate family, and not for the public domain, the result has been a radically privatized eschatology. The purpose of life has been seen entirely in terms of the eternal destiny of the individual human being. In contrast to this, the eschatology of the Bible is a public eschatology. Its focus is not the destiny of the individual but the triumph of Christ in the fulfilment of the purpose of the entire creation. New heavens, a new earth and a holy city are the symbols by which it is described. Certainly, of course, there is an inescapable individual element here. One may, through cowardice and unbelief, miss the way and be lost. But the goal is public, not private. A privatized eschatology fails to send Christians into the public realm; fails to challenge them to see the care and nurture and guidance of the public life of community and nation as an integral part of their responsibility to God; fails therefore to act in the public square in ways which correspond to the reality of what God intends and has promised; fails to unmask effectively the follies which dominate the public square with promises of what cannot be.

The banishing of appeal to divine revelation from the public square leaves the way open for a kind of demoralizing of politics. Most people, indeed, do have a very proper sense that the state is a moral entity in the sense that it can do right or wrong, can act justly or unjustly. Yet, these judgements, which we all make instinctively, imply that there is some criterion by which the actions of the state can be measured. But the dogma of liberalism denies that the state can be committed to any belief which would provide an ontological ground for making judgements of good or bad, right or wrong. Yet in contemporary liberal societies there is a widespread reluctance to allow the state to take sides on moral issues. It is one of the perplexing features of contemporary liberal societies that the moral high ground is claimed by movements of protest rather than the political parties governing or aspiring to govern. The government of a state requires the use of power to coerce and persuade. But there is a strong Manichaean streak in contemporary liberal Christianity which regards all power with suspicion. The pejorative word 'violence' is constantly used to describe the use of power by governments. Those who exercise power in government are generally seen as less morally admirable than those who protest against what is being done. But societies cannot be governed by protest movements. It is sadly true that power tends to corrupt, but without power it is impossible to do good. That is why there is a special obligation upon Christians to pray for those in authority. In the long run the power of those who govern can only be held in check if those who govern acknowledge realities greater than themselves. If it is a matter of accepted public doctrine that these realities are unknowable, it is hard to see by what criteria a particular government can be judged good or bad. It is not without reason that ancient writers regarded democracy as the last station on the line to anarchy and tyranny. As I have said before, it does seem reasonable to hold that the development and persistence of democracy in western Europe has been made possible by the continuing persistence of a residual Christianity among its people, and that as this fades into the pure individualism of the consumer society the future of democracy will become increasingly problematical. This is therefore the place to look at the Judaeo-Christian tradition from which Western liberal democracies have developed.

Israel defines itself as the people of the Torah. Thus Israel is unique among the nations because to Israel alone the God of heaven and earth has made known his will regarding the ordering of human life. This divine will concerns the whole of human life, public and private. Matters which in a modern liberal society would be distinguished from one another as belonging to the categories of politics, law, economics, hygiene, education and religion are all included within the Torah. There is no separation of public from private, as in modern societies. Obedience to the Torah, and therefore the blessing of God, is required of every member of the community, and without this the nation cannot be blessed. Against this background, as set out in the books of the Pentateuch and Joshua, we have the sad stories of disobedience and consequent anarchy. Over and over again the comment is made 'In those days there was no king in Israel; everyone did what was right in his own eyes.' When, as recorded in the first book of Samuel, the demand is made for a king so that Israel may be like the other nations (the 'heathen'), this is seen as rebellion against God, and yet Samuel is instructed to appoint a king, while at the same time warning Israel of the oppression and corruption which kingship will bring with it. The demand for a king is a product of apostasy: if they had obeyed the Torah, they would not have needed a king. So kingship, political power, is something authorized by God but is a sign of human sinfulness. This ambivalence regarding the political order is carried right through into the New Testament, and is vividly illustrated in the contrast between Romans 13, in which the Roman power is portrayed as a ministry ordained by God for the sake of justice, and Revelation 13, where the same power is depicted as a manifestation of Satan. What is clear throughout the story is that the political power is not finally sovereign, that it has its authority from God and is accountable to God. For this reason the Church has, in its main teaching through the centuries, claimed the right to call governments to account. But the intervening pages are full of the agonizing clash between this faith and the huge reality of evil wrought by other powers which seem to flourish in defiance and contempt of God's rule. From beginning to end the Psalms are full of this passionate complaint and protest.

The central theme of the ministry of Jesus is that the decisive moment in this long struggle is imminent, that Israel is being given by God a last chance to fulfil her calling as the bearer of God's truth for all the nations, and that rejection of this opportunity will mean the end of Israel's trusteeship and the destruction of the temple and the holy city. The public ministry of Jesus ended in crucifixion. As a climactic event in the history of Israel this would seem to be the final shattering of Israel's central faith in the kingly rule of God. In his interrogation before the Roman Governor who was finally to order his death, Jesus acknowledged that Pilate's authority was from God, and affirmed that his kingdom was 'not of this world' (John 18.36; 19.11). By this he, as Pilate saw, claimed sovereignty; a sovereignty of a different kind from Pilate's, but one by which Pilate's decision to crucify is judged.

The crucifixion of Jesus was an event on the public stage, seen by all. What followed was an event made known only to a few who had been chosen beforehand and trained over a period of time to understand the nature of Jesus' kingship. Taken by itself, and apart from the apostolic witness to the resurrection, the death of Jesus was the defeat of the rule of God on the plane of public history. If it is taken by itself and apart from what followed, it is the final confirmation of the despair of psalmists who cried in anguish as they experienced the triumph of wickedness in the affairs of men. The resurrection is the manifestation of a reality hidden from an unbelieving world but entrusted to a chosen band of witnesses – namely the ultimate reality of God's triumph. Why is the former event public and the latter a secret entrusted to a few? Because the final vindication of God against a rebellious world could only be the end of history and the destruction of all the doers of evil. There would be no more time or space for repentance and faith. The secret – the open secret, as Paul calls it (Ephesians 3.4–5) – is that God does indeed reign over all his enemies, including the last enemy which is death.

Taken together then, the cross and resurrection assure us that while the final triumph of God's reign is not an event within history (public history) it is nevertheless the final reality, a reality with which everyone will finally have to reckon. But this means that there is a time and space given for repentance and faith, a time in which this good news is to be communicated to all peoples, a time in which all peoples may learn to conform their conduct to that final reality with which they have to reckon at the end. And, of course, this conforming of their conduct refers as much to the conduct of public affairs in the world of politics, economics and culture as to conduct in the more intimate worlds of personal life in home and family. It does not authorize any kind of retreat into 'other-worldliness' if this means a concentration upon the development of one's own soul to the neglect of public duty. On the contrary, it means that those who are called to be the witnesses to Christ's resurrection will be called upon to act in the public sphere in ways which correspond to the real end to which God is directing the life of the world. It will also mean, therefore, that they will be neither surprised nor discouraged if their actions are rejected and scorned by the world, or if they are, in the eyes of the unbelieving world, failures. They will know, because they know of both Jesus' cross and his resurrection, that God in his mysterious way works all things together for good to those who love Him, who are called according to his purpose. They know that God reigns, even though his reign is hidden from unbelieving eyes.

It is this unique event of cross and resurrection that must govern Christian action in the public realm. We have tried to show that the liberal doctrine of religious freedom, when liberal societies are not permeated by the residual power of the Judaeo-Christian tradition, is unable to sustain religious freedom because of its own internal contradiction. Let me summarize this self-contradiction again in its double form. (1) If there is no public doctrine about the nature of ultimate reality, about the ultimate commitments which are the concern of religion, then there is no basis for affirming the liberal doctrine as true against its rivals. (2) If, as a purely secular liberal doctrine holds, there are no supra-natural realities of which we can have knowledge; if, in other words, the observable cosmos and its living inhabitants are all that we can know, then there are no grounds for claiming that the human individual has rights against the collective. The whole is greater than its parts and the latter have no claims against the former.

What is unique about the Christian gospel is that those who are called to be its witnesses are committed to the public affirmation that it is true – true for all peoples at all times – and are at the same time forbidden to use coercion to enforce it. They are therefore required to be tolerant of denial, not in the agnostic sense in which the word 'toleration' is often used; not in the sense that we must tolerate all beliefs because truth is unknowable and all have equal rights. The toleration which a Christian is required to exercise is not something which he must exercise *in spite of* his or her belief that the gospel is true, but precisely *because of* this belief.

This marks one of the very important points of difference between Islam and Christianity. For Islam it is impossible that the cause of Allah should be humiliated and defeated. That is why Muslims, who venerate Jesus, must deny his crucifixion. It would be an inconceivable humiliation of Allah. God must vindicate his honour here within this world's history, even if it takes a long time for this to happen. God's rule must be visibly established and no room must be left for its denial.

One cannot say this without immediately remembering that the empire which early Islam established by military force was, in many respects, the mirror image of the Byzantine Christian empire which it defeated and overran. Both share the assumption that a political order must be based upon something more than the human will and power of those who rule it. And this belief, as we have seen, goes back to the earliest that we know about political power and its legitimation. How can political power endure if its holders can point to nothing beyond their own swords as the reason for obeying them? How can society endure and flourish if there is nothing, no vision, no idea, beyond the conflicting wills of its individual members? Can we be altogether surprised that the utterly new and unprecedented conception of divine power which the gospel introduced was not immediately translated into a new political order? Is it surprising that when the Church inherited responsibility for the Roman Empire in its collapsing condition, it took over much of the ancient tradition of the divine power of the earthly ruler? We have seen how this is expressed in the principle of territoriality: loyalty to the ruling power involves also acceptance of the religion of that power. We have seen how this principle was embodied in the rise of Islam and continues to this day. And we have seen that, in Western Christendom, it was only broken when, as the result of the religious wars of the seventeenth century, it gave way to a new idea of the state as a religiously neutral power offering religious freedom to all citizens. And we have seen how this solution of the ancient problem is showing its inadequacies. Its own assumptions eventually undermine the freedom of conscience which it claims to guarantee.

It is in this long historical perspective that we must look afresh at the idea of a Christian society. There is simply no question of the Church seeking a return to the territorial principle which has been discredited and rejected in the Enlightenment. That move is surely irreversible, and it is simply an evasion of the issue we confront to suggest that it is the only alternative to the present model of a secular society. However difficult it may be, we have to try now, in the light of all we have learned through this long history of Christendom's attempt to relate the gospel to public affairs, to learn what it would mean to affirm the gospel as public truth.

What is offered in the following paragraphs is addressed to the Church. It is not a political programme. Long before we can think of formulating political changes which might be recommended to governments and political parties, there is a need to address Christians about their understanding of the relation of the gospel to the public square. There are, in the first place, some false assumptions to be identified and rejected.

(1) The first concerns the idea of religious neutrality. A state can be religiously neutral in the sense that it does not have to support or to suppress any particular religious belief or practice. This concept of religious neutrality has, as we all know, been classically embodied in the Constitution of the United States of America, which has been the great pioneer and paradigm of the attack on the territorial principle and the development of religious pluralism. But, as has been impressively shown by the writing of Stephen Carter, the effect of this has been to favour non-religious beliefs and practice against religion.[1] Here the problem is with the very term 'religion'. How is this to be defined? In a famous definition, Paul Tillich defined religion as 'ultimate concern'. Whatever is the cause or belief for which you would put everything else aside, that (in this definition) is your religion. In a bizarre case which went to the US Supreme Court, a group of citizens of the State of Arkansas successfully sued a local school board on a charge of violating the Constitution by teaching religion in schools – the religion in question being 'secular humanism'. The case was decided by the Supreme Court in favour of the school board. Everything turns on

the definition of religion. In another case, the court overruled a decision by another state to permit the teaching of 'creation science' along with Darwinism as alternatives. The court decided that the former was 'religion' while the latter was 'science', and this settled the matter.

This judgement highlights the problem in a very clear way. 'Science' is another word for 'knowing' and we have come to use it exclusively for one way of knowing. What is embodied in this and other judgements of the Supreme Court is that one way of knowing is operative in public life and children are required to be trained in it in the state schools, while another way of knowing is a matter for personal and parental choice. Thus the state may be 'religiously neutral' provided we accept a definition of religion (determined by the courts) which separates it from the ways of knowing embodied in 'science'. But the state is not neutral in respect of world-views, meta-narratives or whatever term one may use for the framework which gives overall coherence to our understanding of what it is to be human.

These legal rulings bring to clear sight the fact that the secular liberal society rests in part on the assumption that there is available a body of 'objective' truth which is not a matter of personal or sectarian opinion but is true for all, and has to be understood and accepted by all.

There is today an understanding of the limitations of the scientific method much more widespread than a few decades ago. The nineteenth-century attempt to portray science as the modern replacement for religion as the key to human happiness has faded into the past. There is wider recognition that the methods of science, while brilliantly successful in enabling us to understand how things are produced and function, excludes from its reach the questions of ultimate meaning and purpose. The rise of post-modernism with its scepticism towards all 'meta-narratives' and comprehensive explanations has led also to scepticism regarding the claims of science. But, in spite of these developments, there remains widespread in the popular mind the idea that there is some standpoint from which the claims of religions could be adjudicated and they could be proved to be either true or false. Science is still widely seen as being part of this body of public truth to be acknowledged by all. The effect of this absolutizing of the distinction between two ways of knowing, between science and religion, is (as Stephen Carter shows) to create a bias against religion and to suppress its role in the life of society.

One by-product of this dichotomy between two ways of knowing is the radical difference between the rules which govern inter-religious discussion and those which govern discussion on other matters. In most areas of culture there is vigorous discussion in which the proponents of different views challenge one another and seek to persuade one another. This kind of active debate is the very oxygen which keeps culture alive and fruitful. But different rules are generally applied in the world of interfaith relations. Here 'dialogue' is the order of the day, and the agenda is not a matter of mutual challenge but of sharing and comparing 'experience'. I am not denying all value to this, far from it. Nor am I blind to the dangers of vigorous debate between believers of different faith communities, debates which can easily degenerate into polemics which obscure the truth rather than advance it. But the point is worth making as an illustration of the effect of the removal of religion from the arena of debate about truth.

The first step, therefore, in approaching the idea of a Christian society is a negative one. We have to question the assumption that a secular state is neutral. It does not establish any of the world's religions, but it does establish a world-view which embodies truth-claims which Christians cannot accept and which must be brought into the open and challenged.

This way of understanding the world is very seldom brought out into the open. It is simply assumed because it is the way we are taught to think from our earliest schooldays, and by the unstated assumptions which underlie what we read, watch and hear through the mass media. It is only when we take the difficult step back and reflect from a Christian point of view on what is being said that we recognize what is happening. Our public world is being continually shaped by a certain set of beliefs about what is the case, and these beliefs certainly do not include the belief that the reality with which we finally have to do and to which we shall all finally give an account of our lives, is God as he is made known to us in Jesus Christ. Society is being continually shaped by a set of beliefs which have a privileged position as against other beliefs. We must assume that a Christian society, if such were possible, would be one in which the Christian faith has this privileged position.

(2) The obvious implication of this is that a Christian society would be one in which Christians formed a sufficiently large proportion of the total population to exert a preponderant influence on public life. But this statement needs to be filled out in several respects.

(a) 'Believing the Christian faith' means believing that it is true and is therefore public truth, truth for all, truth which all people ought to accept because it is true. It does not mean taking the Christian faith as a personally preferred option for oneself which, like other personal preferences, we refrain from pressing upon our friends. Once again we must make clear exactly what is being said. We do not seek to impose our Christian beliefs upon others, but this is not because (as in the liberal view) we recognize that they may be right and we may be wrong. It is because the Christian faith itself, centred in the message of the incarnation, cross and resurrection, forbids the use of any kind of coercive pressure upon others to conform. Of course we know, or ought to know, that there are many matters, including matters of religious belief, in respect of which we must recognize that our unbelieving friends may be right and we may be wrong. But our personal commitment to Jesus as Lord and Saviour is not a matter for negotiation or compromise. And it carries with it the obligation to affirm Him as Lord and Saviour of the world, even though we know that we are still faltering and fumbling in our struggle to carry that belief into our daily conduct in the public realm.

(b) This belief carries with it the implication that part of our Christian obedience is the acceptance of our share of responsibility for the life of our city, our nation, the world. This is not an option which one may choose or reject. To ignore it is a dereliction of duty. Here it is necessary to talk about eschatology. During the period when Christianity in both catholic and evangelical forms was flourishing in England (I am thinking especially of the latter half of the nineteenth century), the taunt was often flung at Christians that they offered the victims of the industrial revolution only an other-worldly recompense for their present sufferings, that they offered 'pie in the sky when you die' rather than justice now. This is a gross distortion of the real facts, but it does point to the danger of a privatized eschatology which thinks only of the destiny of the individual soul and not (as the Bible does) of the consummation of God's universal purpose for his whole creation. In the years since the 1914–18 war many Christians have sought to redress the balance by active involvement in issues of social justice and world peace, to the point at which it sometimes becomes difficult to distinguish the Church from a political pressure group. At the present time there is again some reaction.

More and more Christians are tempted to give up hope in the political process, to recognize that the rival promises of political parties are simply empty charades, that there are really no political solutions to our major social ills. There is a danger of retreat into a politically irresponsible concentration on 'religious experience'. The recovery of an authentic and holistic biblical eschatology is essential if we are to speak realistically of a Christian vision for society.

The focus of the biblical vision is on the final vindication of God in the gift of his perfect reign, symbolized in a city of perfect beauty and glory into which all the nations are to bring their honour and glory. This gift of God's blessed reign is both imminent, in the sense that it is the proper horizon of all our actions here and now, whether in the public or the private realms, and at the same time a secret whose timing is wholly in the keeping of God who alone can know what possibilities there remain for repentance, faith and obedience. Our actions do not create this new order, nor do they bring it about. They are, in Albert Schweitzer's fine words, acted prayers to God that he may give us the Kingdom. We act now (in the public realm as in our personal and domestic life) in ways which correspond to the reality which is to be the final reality, the judgement which will be the final judgement. These actions do not directly solve the world's problems. They may fail. They will probably be forgotten after a few years or generations. They are simply committed to God, entrusted to his wise hands, in the faith that nothing entrusted to him is lost. There is an analogy, indeed a continuity here with our most intimate personal acts of discipleship. We know that our mortal bodies will, before many years, be nothing but dust and ashes. Yet we cherish them and care for them, so that they may be instruments useful for God's service for such years as may be given to us. We do not neglect or despise them because they are so transient. So also with the social, political and cultural products of our thought and labour. We are right to recognize that politics will not solve the world's problems. But we would be wrong if we concluded that politics are not part of the substance of Christian discipleship.

(c) The third condition for a Christian contribution to the shaping of society will be that Christians understand the nature of the political order in the way in which the Christian tradition affirms, in spite of the apparent absurdity of talking about 'the Christian tradition' in view of the long history of disagreement among Christians on this matter. Some of our contemporary debates are too much shaped by the fact that Western peoples have been accustomed for so long to living in relatively stable societies where law is administered and enforced in a way which, though open to criticism, is generally accepted. This we have taken for granted. It is when we see such developments as those in Lebanon in the 1980s and in Yugoslavia and Central Africa in the 1990s that we are compelled to see the fact that even a tyrannous and despotic regime can be preferred to chaos and anarchy. In the former situation there are ways by which most individuals can live relatively peaceful lives free from sudden eruptions of violence. When the political order breaks down, peace and security vanish. One can therefore understand, from a purely natural point of view, why St Paul can see even the despotic government of the Roman Empire as a ministry appointed by God. I have already spoken of the ambivalence of the picture of kingship as it is portrayed in the Old Testament, but, in spite of this, the kingship is ordained by God and the king is anointed by God's servant. However many debates may circle around the enigmatic saying of Jesus on the subject of taxes paid to the Emperor Caesar, it is clear, both from this saying and from the words spoken to Pontius Pilate in the story as told by St John (John 19.11) that Jesus acknowledges the authority of the Roman rule as coming from God. Political power is not simply the exercise of brute force by those who have succeeded in crushing their rivals. However political power may have been obtained, those who wield it are responsible to God, and it is the responsibility of the Church to remind them of this fact. When the state fails to use the necessary power to suppress and punish forces of evil and to encourage and sustain movements of good, it fails in its responsibility to God from whom its authority comes.

If we affirm, as I have done, that the function of the state is to punish bad conduct and to reward good conduct, assuming that there are accepted criteria of good and bad, this in turn implies some set of beliefs by reference to which these judgements of good and bad may be made. A state controlled, for example, by Benthamite beliefs will make these judgements in a manner different from a state controlled by Christian beliefs. The idea of neutrality at this point is sheer illusion. All the actions of the state are obviously shaped by the beliefs of those who are, for the time being, in the seats of power, and these in turn reflect, in greater or lesser degree, the beliefs of those who put them in power. In a society where Christians, committed to the truth of their faith and to its expression in the public square, are sufficiently numerous to shape the policy, the state will tend to act upon principles congruent with the Christian faith.

(d) I am assuming that the society of which I speak will be a democratic society. But it will be a democracy shaped more by Christian beliefs than by those of the Enlightenment. It will not see the individual with his or her inalienable rights as the vis-à-vis of the state. When there is nothing between the individual and the state, the inevitable result is the coercion of minorities. A society shaped by Christian beliefs would recognize that, since human being and flourishing is to be understood not in terms of the self-fulfilment of the individual but in terms of the development of interpersonal relationships of trust and responsibility, there will be a multitude of societies intermediate between the individual and the state; places where people meet one another on a face-to-face level and, by argument and persuasion, seek to convince one another about the good and the right. As A. D. Lindsay and others have shown, the deep roots of democracy in England lay in the experience of those Puritan Christians who, in their rejection of the divine right of an autocratic kingship, believed that the will of God could be found in serious engagement with one another under the authority of Scripture.[2] The result hoped for was not simply the rule of the majority over the minority, but the rule of God over all. This is of course a hope which can never be fully realized in a fallen world, but it points to the essential character of a democratic state as Christians would wish to envisage it: a state in which governance is dispersed as widely as possible so that the maximum participation of all in matters of the common good is enlisted.

(3) A third element in the Christian vision for society concerns the role of lay men and women in the life of society and of the Church. From what has been said already, I hope it is clear that Christians ought not to hope for a society controlled by bishops or church synods. The Church can only fulfil its God-given responsibilities by being clearly distinct from the state. The state is required to use coercive power: the Church is forbidden to do so. It is through the presence and activity of committed and competent Christian men and women in the various areas of the common life of society that the Christian vision for society could become effective in practice. The twentieth century has seen a strong anti-clerical movement in most of the churches. The Second Vatican Council has been widely held to mark a watershed in Catholic thinking about the Church as the people of God rather than as a hierarchy of clergy to whom the laity have the duty of humble and unquestioning obedience. In the Anglican and Protestant churches there has been a strong assertion of lay responsibility for the life of the Church and a rejection of clerical dominance. But unfortunately this tends to miss the point. Bishops, priests, and other ordained ministers are set apart for particular functions in enabling the whole Church to fulfil its priestly role as the body of Christ in the world. But the priesthood of the whole membership is not primarily exercised by sitting on church committees or in church assemblies. It is exercised in the life of the world, as the first letter of Peter says, by showing forth the mighty acts of God and by offering up sacrifices worthy of God (1 Peter 2.5, 9). This is to be done in the midst of the life of the world. The reality of the reign of God, hidden from the eyes of unbelievers, is to be made visible to the world through the obedience of believers in the midst of their daily work. The sacrifices acceptable to God are to be made in all the acts of loving obedience, small or great, which a believer is called upon to make in the course of daily work in the world. The priesthood of the people of God is to be exercised in the

midst of the secular world of business, labour, politics and culture. And for this, as the Apostle reminds us, we need to be equipped (Ephesians 4.11–12).

It is here that we must recognize our greatest deficit. In spite of many courageous attempts by groups of Christians, it must be said that in general the Church has not given the necessary attention to equipping all its members for these tasks. To do so is very difficult because we quickly run into sharp differences of judgement. However difficult it may be, the churches must give a very high priority to the development of strategies to help its members in various sectors of public life to form some judgements about their course of action. The long tradition of Catholic social work developed in the past hundred years is one great resource. There are groups of Christians engaged in the worlds of economics, philosophy, literature, medicine and the natural sciences who have worked hard to develop Christian insights into the ways in which these disciplines should develop. But these are only the beginnings, and the Church as a whole has not given to these matters anything like the attention that they need.

In any discussion on the nature of society and of our vision for it, education must have a central place. Societies exist, cohere and flourish in so far as they embody a reasonably coherent understanding of existence within which they can make sense of their personal lives. Education, in its broadest sense, is the initiation of new members of society into this tradition. In contemporary British society the tradition into which young people are initiated in school and college is the set of assumptions which have controlled Western society since the Enlightenment. In a minority of homes – Christian, Islamic, Jewish and others – children are initiated into other traditions. In so far as these are at odds with the tradition into which children are initiated in school and college, they obviously fight a losing battle. Even in homes where the parents are committed Christians, it is hard, to the point of impossibility, for children to sustain belief in the meta-narrative of the Bible over against that understanding of the meta-narrative – the picture of the origins and development of nature, of human society as a whole – which is being offered to them at school. It is possible to maintain the telling of the biblical story in the privacy of home and church, but in so far as this story contradicts the meta-narrative of the schools, young people are placed in an impossible situation. The question 'which is the true story?' must ultimately be faced.

To illustrate the point, one may ask what would be the position of a young scientist who insisted that, whatever the findings of contemporary biologists (always changing) the existence of human life on this earth cannot ultimately be explained without belief in some pre-existing intelligence, and that therefore the neo-Darwinian explanation of the evolution of living organisms and of human beings cannot be the last word on the subject. Such a person would have almost no possibility of appointment and promotion in the academic world. He would be told that such beliefs are permissible as private opinions but that they cannot form part of public opinion. But this *modus vivendi* is ultimately untenable. One has to ask which is true. A belief which is permitted only to exist in a bunker may survive for a time, but it must finally be obliterated. For the sake of the well-being of civil society as a whole, I believe that Christians have a duty to share with those who hold other beliefs, whether religious or secular, to create a public educational system which will train future citizens to live in mutual respect and mutual responsibility while acknowledging their differences in fundamental belief. In this sense I accept what I understand to be the intention of the American writer Os Guiness when he speaks of a 'chartered pluralism'. But this pluralism cannot be sustained if one of these belief systems, namely 'secular humanism', uses its present hegemony to exclude from the curriculum of public education the belief system which is embodied in the Bible. It is only the gospel which enables us to affirm both that the Sovereign Lord of all has made his will and purpose known in Jesus Christ for the whole of our life, private and public, and yet at the same time, not in spite of this but because of this, to affirm that God has ordained a space in which disbelief can have the freedom to flourish. Thus chartered pluralism can only exist where there is a sufficiently large, vigorous and articulate Christian community to sustain the basis on which it rests. To put the same point negatively, if the present erosion of Christian belief continues beyond a certain point, it will become impossible to offer any alternative to the present dominant secularist ideology, since, as I have argued, this ideology is ultimately self-destructive, and the way would be open for other powerful or seductive alternatives.

Perhaps the point can be made clearer by putting it in another way. I have already drawn attention to the fact that the phrase 'a secular society' can be understood in two radically different ways. It may on the one hand refer to a society or an educational system in which different religious beliefs are given equal opportunity to flourish, but may on the other hand refer to a society or an educational system which is dominated by the ideology of secularism, by the belief that all things can be satisfactorily explained without any reference to divine revelation or to any supra-natural realities. I am affirming that in the last analysis it is only the Christian gospel which can sustain a secular society or a secular educational system in the former and proper sense.

A good illustration of what I am trying to suggest has recently been provided by the theologian Gavin D'Costa. His proposal refers to the teaching of theology, religious studies and biblical studies in the universities. At the present time this teaching is almost entirely conducted from within the perspective of what we usually call the modern scientific world-view – in other words, the perspective of post-Enlightenment thought. Teachers in these fields routinely refer to the distinction between what is called 'confessional' theology on the one hand, and 'scientific' or 'academic' theology on the other. The former is regarded as proper only for the church or for institutions exclusively concerned with training Christian ministers and evangelists. Academic theology is taught from a point of view which claims to be above particular confessional commitments. Academic teaching, it is routinely assumed, is free from the bias associated with commitment to any particular religious tradition. All this, of course, conceals the fact that the academic standpoint itself rests upon a commitment to a specific world-view or meta-narrative. It is conceived to be without bias only because it is controlled by the dominant public ideology. What D'Costa proposes is that universities should establish distinct chairs for the teaching of theology. On the one hand there would be teaching which explicitly rests upon commitment to the faith expressed in the Nicene Creed. On the other hand, there would be teaching explicitly resting on the assumptions of post-

Enlightenment thought. The differences would then be open and explicit, held within one forum for questioning, discussion and debate. This, I take it, would be an example of what Os Guiness means by 'chartered pluralism', but once again I would have to affirm that in the long term the only basis on which such an arrangement could be sustained is that provided by the Christian gospel. It is the gospel itself which authorizes freedom of practice of beliefs which are contrary to the gospel.

19

Conclusion: Towards the Good of the City

It is now time to bring the argument of this Part to some kind of conclusion. Is it proper to speak of 'a Christian society'? If by that phrase we mean a society in which the Christian belief so controls all public life as to suppress and exclude alternative beliefs, we must answer that we ought not to have any such goal in mind. The age-long domination of the territorial principle was decisively ended at the Enlightenment, and there can be no going back on that crucial event in the history of the world. Two centuries of religious freedom have taught us so to value it that we can never surrender it. But now, two centuries after the Enlightenment, we are discovering that the principles developed at the Enlightenment cannot in the long run sustain religious freedom. This freedom is increasingly threatened by religious movements which claim absolute control over all life. The only ultimate secure ground for religious freedom is in the fact that Almighty God, in the act of revealing his sovereign power and wisdom in the cross and resurrection of Jesus Christ, has at the same time established for his world a space and a time during which faith is possible because unbelief is also possible. And if we are tempted to cry out to God in impatience because he allows so much wickedness still to flourish in his world, we know that the answer to our cry is in his long, long patience which, as the Apostle tells us, is to lead us to repentance. I am sure that this is the critical point for all debate about the gospel as public truth. Christians agree with Muslims that God's will is to be done in the public no less than in the private sphere. The question is: what kind of obedience does God desire? The central affirmation of the gospel concerning the cross and resurrection of Jesus requires us to affirm that God desires only the freely given, eager, loving obedience of a child who loves and trusts the father. God does not coerce us with the threat of immediate punishment. He woos us, draws us to himself by taking upon himself the awful cost of our disobedience. Certainly the wrath of God against sin is a reality. Certainly God has provided parameters to be policed by the political authority so that our freedom may not lead to total self-destruction. But at the central point, at the point of the ultimate allegiance of the heart, God desires only a freely given obedience which is the expression of love. It follows that while the state with its coercive power has a necessary place in God's wise ordering of the world, for without it our anarchic and disordered wills would destroy the world, yet the state has only a limited mandate. It may not encroach upon that central and secret place where we at our deepest and most intimate are called upon to give our final love and allegiance to our Creator.

But this repentance must lead us to action: action in the public world of which our own personal lives are an integral part and for which we have a responsibility entrusted to us by God. We are, as Jeremiah reminded the exiles in Babylon, to seek the good of the city where we dwell. We are to look for the fruit of the gospel in the public life of society. There is no need for us to be timid or embarrassed about seeking a privileged position for the Christian faith in the public life of the nation. It is obvious that in our present Western societies this privileged position is occupied by another set of beliefs. These beliefs are often, if not very accurately, described as 'secular humanism'. This is not a very satisfactory name for what may perhaps be better called 'naturalism' since the essential point of them is the belief that the whole of reality can be explained without reference to anything beyond the natural world. It is surely beyond question that both in government and in the centres of learning and teaching, it is this set of beliefs which has the privileged position. Particular religious beliefs, such as those of Christians, are only admitted, if at all, by courtesy. More often they are excluded altogether, as many recent events have shown. If we seek, as we ought to seek, a privileged position for the Christian faith in the public domain, this is not, let it be said once again, to exclude or prohibit beliefs but to provide the only foundation upon which freedom of belief is in the long run possible.

Such a privileged position is never won or held except as the result of long intellectual and spiritual struggle. Here I think we come to the heart of the matter. Human society can only flourish if there is vigorous and continuous struggle for the truth. We can never accept, even though we are tempted to do so, the vision of a future state of society in which this struggle is no longer necessary and in which all our different beliefs can simply continue side by side as private opinions. On the basis of the Christian gospel we must affirm that until the coming of Jesus and the end of this present age we are not given the option of living in cosy and secure mental bunkers, but are required to live in the open field where truth and falsehood struggle.

To the end of history we are called upon to be witnesses to the truth in a world where it is contradicted, to engage in the kind of discourse in which through our struggle we learn more of the truth, and always to remain thankful to the God whose providence creates a world in which falsehood can still exist without destroying us. At the end of the season of Promenade concerts in the Albert Hall, which are such a wonderful feature of life in London in the summer and autumn, a huge crowd of mostly young people sing with enormous enthusiasm the words of Blake's poem: 'I will not cease from mental fight, nor shall my sword sleep in my hand, till we have built Jerusalem in England's green and pleasant land.' I often wonder what they think they mean as they join with total abandon in this exhilarating song. Certainly we do not build Jerusalem. The new Jerusalem is a gift from God sent down from heaven, but we are not invited in the gospel merely to sit back and wait for its arrival. We are in that period between Christ's coming and his coming again when we are called upon to put upon us the whole armour of God, and to fight not against human beings ('flesh and blood') but against those spiritual powers which so subtly, and yet often so blatantly, take over the great institutions and movements of public life.

The weapons of this warfare are those which St Paul describes in his letter to the Ephesians. There is first of all the shield of faith, that tough faith which refuses to be intimidated or bamboozled by all the endless attacks upon it which are new in every generation. There is the helmet of salvation, the knowledge of the great reality of God's accomplished work in Jesus Christ which saves us from the temptation to keep our heads down when the weapons are flying around, and enables us to look straight forward and recognize the realities in front of us. There is the sword of the Spirit which is the word of God, the word of God present in Jesus Christ made known to us in the Scriptures, and made powerful and living for this day in the faithful preaching of the word in the power of the Spirit. And above all there is prayer, the prayer of all the faithful, that mighty power which Jesus so often calls us to exercise and to which we can set no limits.

As long as life is given to us on earth we are not permitted to lay aside these weapons. We do indeed look forward with eager longing to that Christian society which is the final goal of all God's creative and redemptive love, but until that day we are called upon to seek on earth a society which, as far as may be granted to us, reflects the glory of the city to which we look forward.

Notes

1 Multiculturalism and Neutrality

1 The word 'pluralism' is used variously in this book in both its general social sense as a fact of apparent religious variety, and as an ideal born out of respect for the cultures and religious beliefs of new migrants and their descendants, to enable them to preserve their distinct identities in a nation that prizes personal freedom. But the word also has a specific theological and philosophical usage with which its other usage is confused. This is epitomized by writers like John Hick, as implying 'a modification [by religions] of their claims to unique superiority in the interests of a more universal conception of the presence of the Real to the human spirit' (See Eliade, *Encyclopedia of Religion*). The debate about multiculturalism follows the same lines.

2 Alain Finkielkraut, *The Undoing of Thought*, London, Claridge Press, 1988.

3 W. E. Gladstone, *The State in its Relation with the Church*, 1843 edn.

2 The Undoing of Secular Society

1 T. S. Eliot, *The Idea of a Christian Society*, London, Faber & Faber, 1939.

2 S. Freud, *Das Unbehagen in der Kultur*, quoted by M. Polanyi in *Personal Knowledge*, London, Routledge & Kegan Paul, 1958, p. 233.

5 The West's Reluctant Re-education

1 Eric Butterworth, *A Muslim Community in Britain*, London, Church Information Service for the Church Assembly Board for Social Responsibility, 1967.

6 Tolerance, Pluralism and Christian Uniqueness

1 Lesslie Newbigin, *The Gospel in a Pluralist Society*, Geneva, World Council of Churches; Grand Rapids Min., Eerdmans, 1989, p. 156.
2 Ibid., p. 157.
3 Ibid., p. 162.
4 Ibid., p. 169.
5 Ibid., p. 178.
6 Ibid., p. 166.
7 Ibid., p. 178.
8 Ibid., p. 179.
9 Ibid., pp. 173–4.
10 Ibid., pp. 177, 180.
11 Ibid., p. 180.
12 Ibid., pp. 181–2.

7 Secular Liberalism and the Muslim Challenge

1 For a succinct, lucid summary see Sir Ernest Barker, *Principles of Social and Political Theory*, Oxford, Clarendon Press, 1951.
2 Arthur Waley, *The Way and Its Power: A Study of the Tao Te Ching and its Place in Chinese Thought*, London, George Allen & Unwin, 1934 (reprinted 1965), Introduction, pp. 69–70. Cited also in Arnold J. Toynbee, *A Study of History*, Abridgement vols. I–VI, Oxford, Oxford University Press, 1987, p. 496.
3 Cited in A. Rippin and J. Knappert (eds), *Textual Sources on Islam*, Manchester, Manchester University Press; and Chicago, Chicago University Press, 1986, pp. 191–2.
4 Cited in G. H. Jensen, *Militant Islam*, London, Pan Books, 1979, pp. 126–7.
5 Nazih Ayubi argues for Islam as 'a religion of collective morals', rather than as 'a particularly political religion'. Nazih Ayubi, *Political Islam: Religion and Politics in the Arab World*, London, Routledge, 1991, p. 120.
6 See W. Montgomery Watt, *Muhammad at Medina*, Oxford, Clarendon Press, 1962, still regarded as the definitive study of the subject.
7 An authoritative Muslim political tract put it as follows: 'the [religious] law of the sultan is the [political] law of the country'. *Usūl al-Siyāsah* (*On the Fundamentals of Government*), reproduced in B. G. Martin, 'A Muslim political tract from northern Nigeria: Muhammad Bello's *Usūl al-Siyāsa*', in Daniel F. McCall and Norman R. Bennett (eds), *Aspect of West African Islam*, vol. 52 Boston, Boston University Press, 1971, pp. 82–3.

8 Cited in Yasir al-Mallah, 'The Relationship of Religion to the State in Islam', *Al-Liqa' Journal*, 3 (May 1994), p. 39. *Al-Liqa'* is a Palestinian review published in Jerusalem by the Center for Religious and Heritage Studies in the Holy Land.
9 Cited in E. I. J. Rosenthal, *Political Thought in Medieval Islam*, Cambridge, Cambridge University Press, 1958, pp. 51ff.
10 Qur'ān 3.104.
11 'Abd al-Masīh ibn Ishāq al-Kindī, *The Apology*, ed. and tr. Sir William Muir, SPCK, London, 1887, pp. 29–30. Al-Kindī, himself a supreme controversialist, added that people turned to Islam in these circumstances, 'some by fear of the sword, some tempted by power and wealth, others drawn by the lusts and pleasures of this life'.
12 Text reproduced in Thomas Hodgkin (ed.) *Nigerian Perspectives: An Historical Anthology*, London, Oxford University Press, 1960, pp. 198ff.
13 Cited in Nizām al-Mulk, *Siyāsat Nāma* (*The Book of Government for Kings*), London, Routledge and Kegan Paul, 1960, p. 63. This work was written in the eleventh century.
14 Cited in H. A. R. Gibb, *Studies on the Civilization of Islam*, ed. Stanford J. Shaw and William R. Polk, London, Routledge & Kegan Paul, 1962, p. 173.
15 At the United Nations Human Rights Conference in Vienna in June 1993, the delegation of the People's Republic of China took the Hobbesian position that 'no rights inhere in persons other than those accorded them by the state'. As reported in Thomas Michel, S. J., 'Differing perceptions of human rights: Asian–African interventions at the Human Rights Conference', in Tarek Mitri (ed.), *Religion, Law and Society*, Geneva, World Council of Churches, 1995, pp. 131–7 (132).
16 John Locke, *A Letter Concerning Toleration*, Buffalo, N.Y., Prometheus Books, 1990, p. 22.
17 Ibid., p. 18.
18 Ibid., p. 19.
19 Ibid., p. 21
20 Ibid., p. 20.
21 Ibid., p. 56.
22 Ibid., p. 56.

8 Caesar Crowned or Turbaned

1 See Mervyn Hiskett, ' "The Song of the Shehu's Miracles": A Hausa Hagiography from Sokoto', *African Language Studies*, 12 (1971).

2 Max Stackhouse, *Public Theology and Political Economy*, Grand Rapids, Eerdmans, 1987, p. 109.
3 Cited in the *Guardian*, 27 January 1986.
4 'Abdullāh al-Ahsan, *OIC: The Organization of the Islamic Conference: An Introduction to an Islamic Political Institution*, Herndon, Va., The International Institute of Islamic Thought, 1988, p. 19.
5 Qur'ān 3:106.
6 Cited in 'Abdullāh al-Ahsan, *OIC*, p. 60.
7 *Digest of Moohummadan Law: Containing the Doctrines of the Hanifeea Code of Jurisprudence*, ed. and tr. Neil B. E. Baillie, 1869–75; reprinted Lahore, Premier Book House, 1974, pp. 169–70.
8 Alexis de Tocqueville, *Democracy in America*, tr. George Lawrence, ed. J. P. Mayer, New York, Harper & Row, 1966, p. 445.
9 In a rambling polemic against the West, a US-based Muslim fundamentalist group claims that for Muslims politics is a sacred duty, and Islamic fundamentalism must assume responsibility for it. 'A political progress for Muslim America', produced by *Muslim America, Inc.*, Olympia, WA 98503.
10 Pat Buchanan, 'The global ascent of Islam', *Colorado Springs Gazette*, 20 August 1989. Pat Buchanan was a Republican presidential candidate in 1992 and again in 1996.

9 Conclusion

1 De Tocqueville, *Democracy*, p. 294.
2 John Dewey, *Freedom and Culture*, Buffalo, Prometheus Books, 1989, p. 125.

10 Cultural Imperialism and the Bradford Riots

1 A. al-Azmeh, *Al-Almaniyya min Manzur Mikhtalif*, Beirut, Markaz Dirasat al-Wahdat al-Arabiyya, 1992, quoted by K. Zebiri in 'Muslim Anti-Secularist Discourse in the Context of Muslim–Christian Relations', *Journal for the Study of Islam and Christianity*, forthcoming.
2 11 March 1996.
3 He answers his own question as to why they come to study in such a pestilential intellectual atmosphere: 'They have to learn western techniques.'
4 'The Changing Context of "Race" in Britain', *Patterns of Prejudice*, 30 (January 1996).

5 Ernest Gellner, *Postmodernism, Reason and Religion*, London, Routledge, 1992, p. 11.
6 Bradford Commission Report (Para. 4.18.5). There are too many references to the report to specify each.
7 Bradford Metropolitan District is the fourth largest of the 36 in England after Birmingham, Leeds and Sheffield. By the year 2000, 50 per cent of school leavers will be Asian (p. 19). Black and Asian population is predicted to grow from 89,000 to 138,000 by 2011 – 'growth of this magnitude is unique in Britain' (p. 19).
8 See contemporary newspaper reports.
9 M. Taj, *A 'Can Do' City: Supplementary Observations, Comments and Recommendations to the Bradford Commission Report*, self-published, 1996, p. 3.
10 Sometimes referred to as 'ethnic entrepreneurs' in multiculturalist discourse.
11 Bradford Commission Report.
12 The Methodist Church and NCH Action for Children, 1997, p. 101. There are signs that language deficiency may become a higher government priority. See the DofEE July 1997 White Paper *Excellence in Schools* especially ch. 3, p. 34. 'People from ethnic minority backgrounds number a tenth of the pupil population and some are at particular risk of under-achieving . . . Over half a million do not have English as a first language and many start school without adequate grasp of it . . .'
13 Figure taken from Bradford Education Welfare Department, 'Prolonged Absence' records.
14 W. Menski, 'Law, religion and South Asians'. Unpublished paper for symposium *A Comparative Study of the South Asian Diaspora Religious Experience in Britain, Canada and the USA*', London, SOAS, 1996, p. 4.
15 Philip Lewis, telephone interviews with the author, 1997.

11 Multiculturalism and the Cult of Silence

1 C. Hamilton, *Family, Law and Religion*, London, Sweet & Maxwell, 1995, pp. 148ff.
2 P. L. Berger, *The Social Reality of Religion*, Harmondsworth, Penguin, 1967, p. 1.
3 'The Vanishing', *The Times Supplement*, 25 August 1996, pp. 11–16.
4 Hannana Siddiqui, Southall Black Sisters, quoted in 'The Vanishing'.
5 Ibid., p. 16.
6 Taj, *A 'Can Do' City*, p. 3.
7 See L. Green, 'Internal Minorities and their Rights', in W. Kymlicka

(ed.), *The Rights of Minority Cultures*, Cambridge, Islamic Text Society, 1995, pp. 258ff.

8 A. Finkielkraut, *The Undoing of Thought*, London and Lexington, Claridge Press, 1988, p. 73.

9 Ibid., p. 74.

10 *The History of al-Tabari*, vol. IX, *The Last Years of the Prophet*, tr. J. Poonawala, New York, State University Press, 1990, pp. 128ff. Also M. Lings, *Muhammad: His Life Based on the Earliest Sources*, London, Islamic Texts Society, 1983, p. 106.

11 Quoted from *'al-Ihya 'Ulum al-Din'*, in Kenneth Cragg, *The Call of the Minaret*, New York, Oxford University Press, 1956, p. 92. See also Suzanne Haneef, *What Everybody should Know about Islam and Muslims*, Lahore, Kazi Publications, 1979, p. 25.

12 Menski, 'Law, religion and South Asians', p. 16.

12 Religion, Law and Social Policy

1 Menski, 'Law, religion and South Asians'.

2 Quoted in Anthony Bradney, *Religions, Rights and Laws*, Leicester, Leicester University Press, 1993, p. 4.

3 See S. Spencer (ed.), *Strangers and Citizens: A Positive Approach to Migrants and Refugees*, IPPR/Rivers Oram Press, 1994, passim.

4 Ibid., p. 3.

5 L. Fransman, 'Future Citizenship Policy', in Spencer, *Strangers and Citizens*, p. 291.

6 The 'source of lineage' for his view is the 1689 Toleration Act which allowed non-Conformist Trinitarian Protestants to worship, provided the doors were kept open (this did not apply to Roman Catholics). It introduced the principle in law that a person might be excused penalty on the grounds of the dictates of their religious conscience.

7 Bradney, *Religions, Rights and Laws*, p. 6.

8 Muslim lobby groups recognize this: a campaign to get a question of religious affiliation in the 2001 Census is part of a drive to 'put Muslims on the demographic map'. *Q News*, 15 November 1996.

9 W. Menski, 'Sharī'ah Law', London, School of Oriental and African Studies, 12 March 1997.

10 Quoted in T. Asad, *Genealogies of Religion*, Baltimore and London, Johns Hopkins University Press, 1993, p. 258.

11 Sikhs do not have legal status as a distinct racial group in India.

12 Menski, 'Law, religion and South Asians', p. 6.

13 R. Ballard, 'Racial inequality and ethnic diversity and social policy: pre-

requisites for the professional delivery of public services'. Unpublished paper presented at SOAS Seminar, 1996, footnote 8.

14 W. A. R. Shadid and P. S. van Koningsveld, *Religious Freedom and the Position of Islam in Western Europe: Opposition and Obstacles*, Kampen, Kok Pharos, 1995, p. 82.

15 Another writer, S. Poulter, 'Multiculturalism and human rights for Muslim families in English law', in M. King (ed.), *God's Law Versus State Law: The Construction of an Islamic Identity in Western Europe*, London, Grey Seal, 1995, p. 83.

16 *Hypotheticals*, Granada TV, 1989. Death for blasphemy is law, following a *hadith*, in Pakistan where under the Penal Code it is mandatory, once proven.

17 Bradford Commission Report (Para. 5.21.11, p. 103).

18 R. Ballard (ed.), *Desh Pardesh: The South Asian Presence in Britain*, London, Hurst, 1994, p. 1. (My own view is that future historians may well conclude that the impact of the arrival of South-Asian and Afro-Caribbean settlers on the British social and cultural order will eventually prove almost as great as that precipitated by the arrival of William of Normandy in 1066.)

19 Cited in MAB prayer letter, 1 March 1997.

20 Ballard, 'Racial inequality', p. 2.

21 See P. Pelto and G. H. Pelto, 'Studying knowledge, culture and behavior in applied medical anthropology', *Medical Anthropology Quarterly*, 11.2 (June 1997), pp. 147ff.

22 Ibid.

23 Ballard, 'Racial inequality', p. 6.

24 '. . . Vaughan Robinson in *Transients, Settlers and Refugees*, (OUP, 1986), the most ambitious attempt so far to inject some methodological rigour into the subject, omits any reference to religion in his subject index.' P. Lewis, 'Being Muslim and being British', in Ballard, *Desh Pardesh*, p. 58.

25 Ballard, *Desh Pardesh*.

26 Ibid., p. 11.

27 See S. Sutcliffe (ed.), *Aisha My Sister*, Carlisle, Solway, 1997. Documents case studies of Muslim women converts' difficulties.

28 P. Werbner, 'The fiction of unity in ethnic politics', in P. Werbner and M. Anwar (eds.) *Black and ethnic Leaderships in Britain: The Cultural Dimensions of Political Action*, London, Routledge, 1991, pp. 113–45.

29 Ibid., p. 131.

30 Ibid., p. 132.

31 Ibid, p. 140.

32 Ibid., p. 130.

33 Before the 1997 General Election, the UK Action Committee on Islamic Affairs, in urging Muslims to exercise their vote, took a more 'British' approach to political participation than did the Muslim Parliament, who urged a Muslim boycott.

34 Dick Caborn, at the time of writing.

35 Robert Key addressed the C of E Synod in 1991, calling for a new partnership between church and state.

36 Paul Beresford, interview conducted at the Department of the Environment, London, 31 October 1996.

37 Newcastle's total ethnic minority population is 4 per cent. Of these 20.1 per cent live in Elswick, which has a 22.5 per cent ethnic population. Figures are taken from doctoral research by Ida Glaser, Crosslinks Other Faiths Coordinator.

38 Methodist Church with NCH Action for Children, *The Cities*, 1997, p. 25.

39 B. Robson, *Assessing the Impact of Urban Policy*, HMSO, 1994, quoted in *The Cities*.

40 In urban policy circles, 'black' is used sometimes for Afro-Caribbean, sometimes for all 'people of colour', including Asian. *The Cities* does not define its use of the term.

41 'Changes have taken place in recent years, such that some of the population are designated by, and describe themselves in terms of, religion. This is at present notably the case for some followers of Islam . . . very little of our subject matter is best described by using descriptions of people's religious loyalties' (Bradford Commission Report, Para 1.7.11). This is a signal misreading of the nature of 'identity' among non-secular people for whom identity is integral with religion. Such a misreading constitutes the general failure to perceive 'difference' – or, as Ballard puts it, more astringently, 'white myopia that reduces non-European others to nothing more than Blacks' (Ballard, Unpublished).

13 An Islamic Vision for Britain?

1 Muhammad Khalid Masud discusses the problems for modern Muslims in the West. According to classical Muslim jurists, he says, '[a] Muslim living in dar al-kufr is religiously obligated to migrate to dar al-Islam'. *Journal of the Institute of Muslim Minority Affairs*, January 1989, p. 119.

2 'The Islamic policies of the Western colonial powers: their relevance in the European Union in the post-colonial era', South Asian Studies

Annual Lecture, School of Oriental and African Studies, London University, 6 November 1996.

3 Kalim Siddiqui, *The Muslim Manifesto: A Strategy for Survival*, London, Muslim Institute, 1990, p. 31.

4 Larry Poston refers to it extensively in *Dawah in the West*, Cambridge, Cambridge University Press, 1992.

5 *Q News*, 7 February 1997.

6 See the informative discussion in J. Esposito (ed.), *Oxford Encyclopaedia of the Modern Islamic World*, 1995, pp. 343ff.

7 M. M. Pickthall, *The Meaning of the Glorious Qur'an: An Explanatory Translation*, London, Ta Ha, 1930.

8 Ron Geaves' thesis *Sectarian Influences within Islam in Britain*, Leeds University of Leeds Community Relations Project, 1996, makes a most important contribution to this new field while admitting that the wider influence of Jamaat-i-Islami on Muslims who are non-members in Britain is unresearched.

9 See his 'Sociological analysis of Jamaat-i-Islami in the United Kingdom', in R. Barot (ed.), *Religion and Ethnicity: Minorities and Social Change in the Metropolis*, Kampen, Kok Pharos, 1993, p. 77.

10 C. J. Adams, 'The ideology of Mawlana Maududi', in D. E. Smith (ed.), *South Asian Politics and Religion*, Princeton, Princeton University Press, 1969; M. Jameela 'An appraisal of some aspects of Maulana Sayyid Ala Maudoodi's life and thought', *Islamic Quarterly* (1987) pp. 116–30.

11 Geaves, *Sectarian Influences*, p. 223.

14 Religious Rights and the Sharī'ah

1 Ayubi, *Political Islam*, p. 35.

2 Ibid.

3 See S. Poulter's chapter, 'The claim to a separate Islamic system of personal law for British Muslims', in C. Mallat and J. Connors (eds), *Islamic Family Law*, London, Graham and Trotman, 1990.

4 Ibid.

5 'Race watchdog is against Muslims', *Guardian*, 20 September 1995. 'The secular nature of the CRE has completely discredited it within the Muslim community,' said Fuad Nahdi, editor of *Q News*.

6 J. D. Eller, 'Anti-anti-multiculturalism', *American Anthropologist*, 99 (1997) – an important essay from a secular standpoint on whose worries are more justifiable: those of the advocates or opponents of multiculturalism?

15 Secularization and Assimilation

1 'Assumption 5', *The Muslim Manifesto: A Strategy for Survival*, London, The Muslim Institute, 1990. Such resistance is more than prescriptive. The PSI study into assimilation, *Ethnic Minorities in Britain*, published in 1997, revealed that 51 per cent of Pakistanis would mind if a close relative were to marry a white person, against 12 per cent of Caribbeans, or 25 per cent of white people marrying a non-white.

2 al-Azhar University, Cairo, the oldest and most prestigious Islamic university.

3 Zaki Badawi, *Third Way*, May 1996, pp. 16–19.

4 'The Changing Context of Race in Britain', *Patterns of Prejudice*, 30 (January 1996), p. 12.

5 Interview with the author. 'A political creed?' *Third Way*, March 1996.

6 S. S. Husain and S. A. Ashraf, *Crisis in Muslim Education*, Sevenoaks, Hodder & Stoughton, 1979, p. 2.

7 Ibid., p. 57.

8 S. Barton, *The Bengali Muslims of Bradford*, Leeds, University of Leeds Community Relations Project, 1986, p. 182.

9 K. Cragg, *Sandals at the Mosque*, London, SCM Press, 1995, pp. 48–9.

10 Husain and Ashraf, *Crisis in Muslim Education.*

11 W. A. Shadid and P. S. van Koningsveld, *The Integration of Islam and Hinduism in Western Europe*, Kampen, Kok Pharos, 1991.

12 A. Shaw, *A Pakistani Community in Oxford*, Oxford, Blackwell, 1988, pp. 177–8.

13 D. Joly, *Britannia's Crescent: Making a Place for Muslims in British Society*, Aldershot and Vermont, Avebury, 1995, p. 183.

14 Shadid and van Koningsveld, *Integration of Islam and Hinduism*, p. 7.

15 P. Lewis, *Islamic Britain: Religion, Politics and Identity among British Muslims*, London and New York, I. B. Tauris, 1995, passim.

16 Shaw, *Pakistani Community in Oxford*, p. 147.

17 See Jahangir Mohammed, *The Home Office Strategy for Islam and Muslims in Britain*, London, Muslim Parliament of Great Britain.

18 Multiculturalists argue that there is an emotional danger in that groups, excluded by a Eurocentric focus, develop negative self-image and low self-esteem and are therefore less likely to succeed. (See Eller, 'Anti-anti-multiculturalism'.)

19 Tariq Modood, 'Establishment, multiculturalism and British citizenship', *Political Quarterly*, 65 (January–March 1994), pp. 53–73.

20 The role of the Church as 'broker' to other faiths in pastoral care, chaplaincies and civic religion was the subject of a recent research

project undertaken by Sophie Gilliat in the Department of Sociology at Warwick University, initiated by the Archbishop of Canterbury, George Carey.

16 Islamophobia and the Church

1 P. Lewis in an interview with the author for *Third Way*, May 1997.
2 Max Weber, *The Protestant Ethic and the Spirit of Capitalism*, 1905, tr. T. Parsons, London, Routledge, 1992, p. 182.
3 *Hansard*, 4 December 1985.
4 Interviewed by the author for 'A political creed', *Third Way*, March 1996.
5 A letter submitted by *Q News* to the CRE, 31 January 1992: 4 said: 'The [1976] Act has been the one major cause for the deprivation, alienation and marginalisation of Britain's Muslim community.'
6 T. Modood, 'Muslim views on religious identity and racial equality', *New Community*, April 1993, p. 518.
7 R. Ballard, 'Islam and the Construction of Europe', in *Muslims on the Margins*, Kok Pharos, 1996, p. 50.

17 The Demoralizing of Politics

1 I. S. Markham, *Plurality and Christian Ethics*, Cambridge, Cambridge University Press, 1994.
2 A. van Leeuwen, *Christianity and World History*, London, Edinburgh House, 1994, pp. 195ff.

18 Activating the Christian Vision

1 S. L. Carter, *The Culture of Disbelief*, New York, HarperCollins, 1993.
2 A. D. Lindsay, *Essentials of Democracy*, London, Oxford University Press, 1935.

The Society for Promoting Christian Knowledge (SPCK) was founded in 1698. It has as its purpose three main tasks:

- **Communicating the Christian faith in its rich diversity**
- **Helping people to understand the Christian faith and to develop their personal faith**
- **Equipping Christians for mission and ministry**

SPCK Worldwide serves the Church through Christian literature and communication projects in over 100 countries. Special schemes also provide books for those training for ministry in many parts of the developing world. SPCK Worldwide's ministry involves Churches of many traditions. This worldwide service depends upon the generosity of others and all gifts are spent wholly on ministry programmes, without deductions.

SPCK Bookshops support the life of the Christian community by making available a full range of Christian literature and other resources, and by providing support to bookstalls and book agents throughout the UK. SPCK Bookshops' mail order department meets the needs of overseas customers and those unable to have access to local bookshops.

SPCK Publishing produces Christian books and resources, covering a wide range of inspirational, pastoral, practical and academic subjects. Authors are drawn from many different Christian traditions, and publications aim to meet the needs of a wide variety of readers in the UK and throughout the world.

The Society does not necessarily endorse the individual views contained in its publications, but hopes they stimulate readers to think about and further develop their Christian faith.

For further information about the Society, please write to:
SPCK, Holy Trinity Church, Marylebone Road,
London NW1 4DU, United Kingdom.
Telephone: 0171 387 5282